AMERICA AND THE JACKSONIAN ERA
1825–1850

America and the Jacksonian Era 1825–1850

FON W. BOARDMAN, JR.

HENRY Z. WALCK, INC.   *New York*

Library of Congress Cataloging in Publication Data

Boardman, Fon Wyman, 1911–
    America and the Jacksonian era, 1825–1850.

    Bibliography: p.
    Includes index.
    SUMMARY: Discusses the second quarter of the
nineteenth century in its various aspects including
political, social, and cultural.
        1. United States—Politics and government—
1825–1850—Juvenile literature. 2. United States—
Civilization—19th century—Juvenile literature.
[1. United States—Politics and government—
1825–1850. 2. United States—Civilization—19th
century]   I. Title.
E338.B6   973.5   75-6019
ISBN 0-8098-3128-7

MANUFACTURED IN THE UNITED STATES OF AMERICA

Contents

AMERICA AND THE JACKSONIAN ERA
1825–1850

1 An Era Begins

THE TALL, gaunt man with stiff white hair and piercing eyes, dressed in somber black in memory of his recently deceased wife, walked from Gadsby's Hotel to the Capitol in Washington, D. C., to be inaugurated seventh president of the United States. It was March 4, 1829, a sunny day, when Andrew Jackson—within two weeks of his sixty-second birthday and famous for many years as an Indian fighter and as hero of the War of 1812—took the oath of office. An immense crowd of people who had come from all over the country thronged the Capitol area to see and hear, and perhaps to touch, their hero. They saw him, but not many heard him for he delivered his brief inaugural address in a low voice.

Nevertheless, the people cheered and followed their hero in an informal parade as he rode to the White House in a carriage. There the common people, uninvited but made welcome, took over the reception, paying no heed to high-ranking officials and diplomats. Andrew Jackson represented, in his followers' eyes, the true democracy of America, and that democracy had triumphed. They came to celebrate the triumph, which they did, standing on chairs and jamming the rooms so that men and women were trampled and glassware and china broken. The new president, despite the efforts of friends to shield him, was so jammed against a wall that only with difficulty was he eased out a back door before his supporters overwhelmed him.

Andrew Jackson (1767–1845), born in South Carolina a month after his father died, was a schoolboy when he was caught up in the American Revolution. Riding with American troops in 1780, he and his brother were captured by the British. A British officer struck him with a sword when he refused to clean the officer's boots, and in a prison camp Jackson caught smallpox. Eventually he was freed and recovered. Four years later he began to study law and in 1787 was admitted to the bar. Finding little opportunity in the Carolinas, for a young lawyer, he set out for Tennessee the next year.

Like other ambitious young men of the time, Jackson found room for his talents in the new and growing America west of the Allegheny Mountains. Here one could start with nothing and achieve both economic and social standing within a few years. Jackson settled in Nashville, began his rise both as a lawyer and a landowner, and in 1788 fought the first of a number of duels (both men missed). In 1791 Jackson began to put down roots by marrying and, in 1795, by buying the land that became his gracious and impressive estate, the Hermitage. The marriage, however, was troubled by an unusual situation. Jackson's bride was Mrs. Rachel Donelson Robards, who understood that her husband had divorced her. As the couple found out two years later, it was not until that date that the divorce actually took place. All his life, Jackson's enemies made the most of this "scandal."

As a landowner and a farmer, Jackson began by building a log cabin, as did other pioneers whose successful careers made them a new aristocracy. The cabin was to be replaced in 1819 by a brick mansion, which later was enhanced by a formal garden. Consisting of 640 acres, the Hermitage was a working farm where eighty slaves grew cotton, corn and other crops.

Andrew Jackson was imposing in appearance as well as in accomplishment. An inch over six feet tall, he was thin and, as he grew older, gaunt. He always stood straight, walked with a firm step and, all in all, presented a commanding appearance, which was backed by his personality and his actions. As he grew older, his wounds and illnesses took their toll in his appearance and his movements, but he gave in to them as little as possible. He had a reputation among those who disliked him for high-handed action, and for being rude and obstinate. His followers saw him as a resolute man of spirit and firm purpose. He was strong-willed and strong-tempered, but he could be sentimental and kind, as witnessed by his love for his wife and the adoption of eleven children, one of them an Indian baby.

Jackson became active in politics at an early age. When Tennessee became a state in 1796, he was elected as its first member of the House of Representatives. The following year he was elected to the Senate, but resigned in 1798, preferring to become a judge in Tennessee where he could keep in better touch with his own business affairs. Jackson's eye next fell on the position of major general of the state militia. Under the system then in effect, the officers of the militia chose their commander, and Jackson won a close and acrimonious contest to become a general at the age of thirty-five. In the course of the next few years, his chief use of arms was in a duel with Charles Dickinson in 1806, an affair that started with a dispute over a wager on a horse race. Both men hit their targets, Dickinson bleeding to death and Jackson receiving a bullet in his chest which remained there all his life.

The War of 1812 made a military hero of Jackson. In command of the Tennessee militia, he was sent to chastise the Creek Indians in the south. This he did in March, 1814, shattering the Creek power at the battle of Horseshoe Bend, Alabama. For this action he was made a major general in the United States Army and his troops dubbed him "Old Hickory" because of his toughness. He also created another incident his enemies were to use against him in later years by having several alleged deserters shot. Later in 1814, when a British attack on New Orleans was expected, Jackson was put in command of the city's defenses. With an assortment of Kentucky and Tennessee riflemen, some free-Negro soldiers and the followers of the pirate Jean Lafitte, the general arranged a well-protected line and awaited the assault of veteran British troops who had fought against Napoleon under the Duke of Wellington. On the morning of January 8, 1815 (two weeks after a treaty of peace had been signed in Europe but before word could reach the United States), 5,000 British troops advanced on the American positions, only to be beaten back by the accurate fire of Jackson's men. The British left more than two thousand dead, while American losses were only eight killed and thirteen wounded.

After the war, Florida, a Spanish possession, was a refuge for hostile Indians who threatened the border areas of the southern states. To get rid of this nuisance, General Jackson was again ordered into action. With his troops he marched into Florida in the spring of 1818 and subdued the Indians. He also seized two Spanish towns, which he had not been authorized to do, hung one British citizen and had another shot because, he said, they were aiding the Indians. British newspapers denounced Jackson as a "ruffian" and in the House of Representatives Henry Clay led an attack on his actions, but the public seemed to approve. When Florida became part of the United States, the general was appointed the first territorial governor but resigned after less than a year. As early as 1822, the Tennessee legislature nominated Jackson as a candidate for president in the election to be held in 1824, and in December, 1823, the same legislature elected him to the Senate.

But the hero of the frontier and of the common people was not destined to be president just yet. The Republican party (unrelated to the present-day Republicans) which had come to power with Thomas Jefferson in 1800 was the only party, but it was split into a number of factions. As a result, four men contended for the presidency, even after John C. Calhoun dropped out of the race in order to run for vice-president. Besides Jackson, they were John Quincy Adams (1767–1848), William H. Crawford (1772–1834) and Henry Clay (1777–1852). Adams was the son of the second president, John Adams, and carried on the Puritan tradition of Massachusetts. Crawford, from Virginia, had been a senator and had held several cabinet positions.

Clay, born in Virginia and long a leader in Kentucky, was ten years younger than Jackson but had already served in the national government in several posts for a quarter of a century. As early as 1811 he was speaker of the House of Representatives, and foremost among the "War Hawks" who led the country into the War of 1812.

Crawford's candidacy faded after he suffered a stroke, and Clay had little backing outside Kentucky. The race was primarily between Jackson and Adams, and the former received the most popular votes—about 156,000 to 105,000. In the Electoral College no one had the required majority. Jackson won ninety-nine; Adams, eighty-four; Crawford, forty-one; and Clay, thirty-seven. Under the provisions of the Constitution, this threw the election into the House where its members, voting by states, would select the new president from among the top three candidates. Clay was thereby eliminated and gave his support to Adams, who was chosen in February, 1825, by the vote of thirteen states—the minimum necessary out of the twenty-four in the Union. Jackson and his followers considered themselves robbed, and when Adams named Clay to be secretary of state, they charged a deal had been made, but no evidence to this effect was produced. The election marked the end of the Republican party, which divided in two. The Adams-Clay faction became the National Republicans (later the basis of the Whig party), while Jackson's followers formed the Democratic Republican party (later the Democratic party).

John Quincy Adams did not look the part of a leader as did his rival Jackson, but no man was a more devoted public servant. Adams was unprepossessing, being short and stout, with a large bald head. He was not easygoing in company and spent almost all his time on public business. Among his few recreations was swimming in the Potomac, which he did regularly and in the nude. As a young man Adams accompanied his father abroad on diplomatic missions. Later he too served abroad, and in 1803 was elected to the Senate. He succeeded to the presidency from the position of secretary of state, which he had filled wisely and with distinction. Adams, in fact, had been the chief author of the Monroe Doctrine which his predecessor, President James Monroe, proclaimed in 1823.

Adams became president of the United States as the nation entered the second quarter of the nineteenth century. It was a steadily growing and expanding nation, the census of 1820 having recorded 9,638,000 people. About a quarter of the population lived west of the Alleghenies; by 1830 the figure reached nearly one third. In that decade, Ohio's population, for example, grew from 581,434 to 937,903 and Mississippi's from 75,448 to 136,621. The number of cities with a population of 8,000 or more increased from 11 to 24.

The Federal government was also growing. Government expenses were around $20,000,000 in 1825, but increased each year until the depression of 1837. Fortunately, government revenues, chiefly from the tariff and the sale of public lands, kept going up also. The political climate was changing as the nation moved steadily toward universal white manhood suffrage. The secret ballot did not exist yet, but in 1824 only six states still chose presidential electors through the legislature. In general, landowners, capitalists, planters and the well-to-do of the South and East were losing political power, while the working class in the cities and the frontier farmers were gaining.

Adams did not fit into this changing scene of new political forces and new parties. Although programs he proposed were well suited to the times, they were mostly rejected by Congress. In his first message to Congress he proposed internal improvements, such as the building of roads and canals. He was especially interested in science, and recommended scientific expeditions and a revision of the patent laws, but Congress ignored him. He displeased his supporters by not removing opponents from government positions so as to give places to his friends. In the midterm elections of 1826, the Democrats, operating for the first time as a national political party, won a majority in both houses of Congress. Adams thought political parties were bad and that Americans should and could unite on a common program. He was out of step with his era, for this was the beginning of a period of parties held together by loyalty to leaders and policies, presenting a united front in order to carry out programs and to win the benefits of government jobs and other favors. Practical goals, rather than political ideals, governed party action.

Adams was no more successful in foreign affairs than in domestic. When Simon Bolivar, the military leader who freed several Latin American countries from Spanish rule, called a congress of all the nations of the hemisphere to meet in Panama in 1826, Adams recommended that the United States participate. Opposition in Congress was strong and mostly political. Congress eventually approved sending two delegates, but one died en route, and the other got only as far as Mexico City before the Panama Congress adjourned without accomplishing anything.

The presidential election of 1828 was a rematch between Adams and Jackson, and was the dirtiest presidential campaign to that time. No one debated public issues. Adams had his following in the conservative North. Jackson was the popular hero of the common people everywhere. Adams, who had bought a billiard table and chess set for the White House at his own expense, was accused by the Democrats of using public funds to buy gambling equipment. National Republicans again charged Jackson with unjustly having had six soldiers shot for desertion in 1814. They also spread again the story of his having lived with Rachel before her divorce. The total vote reached 1,157,000, compared with a little more than 350,000 in 1824. Jackson received 647,000 popular votes to Adams's 510,000, and 178 votes to 83 in the Electoral College. Voting followed class lines more than anything else, as Jackson carried the West and the South, Pennsylvania and New York, while Adams won in the rest of the North. Jackson's inauguration in March, 1829, marked the first substantial change in control of the Federal government since Jefferson defeated John Quincy Adams's father in 1800.

Except for Martin Van Buren of New York, whom he named secretary of state, Jackson's official cabinet was not particularly distinguished. More influential, especially in the first two years of the administration, were some political friends and newspaper editors who were soon called the "Kitchen Cabinet." Chief among them were Francis P. Blair (1791–1876), Amos Kendall (1789–1869) and Duff Green (1791–1875). It was customary for each administration to have a newspaper that was accepted as its official "mouthpiece." Blair, who was born in Virginia and was a successful newspaper editor in Kentucky, was brought to Washington in December, 1830, to edit a new pro-Jackson paper, the *Washington Globe*. He also advised Old Hickory on political matters.

Kendall also was a leading journalist in Kentucky. He was born in Massachusetts and originally went to Kentucky as tutor to the children of Henry Clay. Kendall wrote many of Jackson's state papers, and was an influential strategist in the political battles of the time. Appointed postmaster general in 1835, he reorganized the department, which needed it badly. Green, another journalist and politician, was born in Kentucky and moved to Washington in 1825. There he purchased the *United States Telegraph* and made that paper a Jackson organ. However, he gradually switched his loyalties from Jackson to the south and its leading spokesman, John C. Calhoun.

Two squabbles, one an affair of social prestige, the other a political matter, and both involving the influential Calhoun, marred Jackson's first two years in office. The social affair concerned Margaret (Peggy) O'Neale (1796–1879). Peggy was the pretty and witty daughter of a boardinghouse keeper, one of whose long-time boarders was Senator John H. Eaton (1790–1856). Peggy was married, but gossip asserted that she was Eaton's mistress. When her husband died in 1828, Senator Eaton married her, with Jackson's blessing. Old Hickory, who named Eaton as his secretary of war, thought this would stop the gossip, but it didn't. Vice-president Calhoun's wife refused to receive Eaton's bride and others followed suit. Only Van Buren, a widower, supported Jackson, who refused to disavow the couple.

Calhoun and Van Buren were already maneuvering for favor with Jackson, each hoping to receive Jackson's blessing as his successor.

The falling-out of Jackson and Calhoun became final in 1831. On the basis of several pieces of evidence, the president became convinced that Calhoun, when a member of President Monroe's cabinet, had voted to censure Jackson for his actions in Florida in 1818. Calhoun did his best to give the impression this was not true. When accused directly, Calhoun published a lengthy and unconvincing reply. This boomeranged on him within the Democratic party and Van Buren used it to gain ascendancy over the vice-president.

In 1829, in his first message to Congress, Jackson spoke out for rotation in office so far as government jobs were concerned. The duties of public officers, he said, were "plain and simple," and "no one man has any more intrinsic right to official station than another." He proposed that all government appointments be limited to four years. While Jackson was sincere, great pressure was put on him to reward his followers by dismissing men appointed under previous administrations and replacing them with staunch Democrats. The new politics of permanent, organized parties required more men who were prepared to spend large amounts of time working for their party. They believed they had a right to government posts if they helped their party win.

The combination of Jackson's stand for rotation in office and the complete changeover in control of the Federal government in 1829 has left Jackson with the reputation of inaugurating the "spoils system" in American government. The term was coined by William L. Marcy (1786–1857) in an 1832 Senate speech when he proclaimed that "to the victor belong the spoils." Marcy was a leading figure in the Albany Regency, the name given to the dominant group, headed by Van Buren, which created the powerful Democratic party machine in New York State. Jackson, in the course of two terms, replaced only about 20 per cent of Federal job holders for political reasons.

Some of the events of Jackson's first term concerned public works,

West Indian trade and imprisonment for debt. When Congress in 1830 passed a bill providing for government construction of a road between Maysville and Lexington, in Kentucky, Jackson vetoed it. He declared that if the people wanted the Federal government to do such things, a constitutional amendment was necessary. This Maysville veto made Jackson seem more in the states' rights camp than he actually was. He later approved other similar projects. The veto was really aimed at Henry Clay of Kentucky, leader of the National Republicans.

The Jackson administration's first successful move in foreign affairs concerned trade with the British West Indies. Great Britain restricted American trade with the islands, while the United States would not allow American goods to be sent there in British ships. Adams refused to compromise, but in 1830 both sides were ready to reach an agreement, and by October Jackson was able to proclaim unrestricted trade between the United States and the islands.

Jackson also reversed his predecessor's policy in the matter of imprisonment for debt. For many years, working people had fought the laws which allowed creditors to have a person jailed for debt. In 1829 one estimate indicated that 75,000 persons, more than half of whom owed less than twenty dollars, were jailed each year. In some cases widows with children, and old and infirm persons were behind bars for debts of less than one dollar. Adams had opposed a change, but in 1832 the Jackson administration put through a bill that ended imprisonment for debt in Federal court actions. Within ten years almost all the states followed suit.

Such matters, however, were minor compared with the controversies involving the nullification of Federal law by a state, and the rechartering of the Bank of the United States, which showed Jackson at his most obstinate.

2 Jackson: Nullification and the Bank

JACKSON WAS the center of two political controversies during his first term, and he triumphed in both by showing unrelenting firmness. One, the nullification issue, threatened to split the Union; the other, the debate over granting the Second Bank of the United States a new charter, deepened the gulf between the two political parties and between the common people on the one hand and the business and financial world on the other.

Of the two, nullification was the more serious and the more lasting in its effects. Nullification involved the question of states' rights, a question that had been fiercely debated even before the Constitution was adopted. Was the Federal government an all-powerful central government, representing the people of all the states, or was it a compact among the sovereign states, each of which had the right to decide whether to obey Federal law? The showdown on nullification grew out of the tariff acts of 1828 and 1832, but the basic issues were brilliantly illuminated in the Webster-Hayne debate of 1830, over an entirely different legislative matter. It was, perhaps, the finest debate ever heard in the Congress of the United States.

The Webster-Hayne confrontation began with the introduction of a resolution by Senator Samuel A. Foot (1780–1846) of Connecticut in December, 1829. Senator Foot wanted the Senate to instruct the committee on the public lands to consider restricting the sale of such land. The people of the West, and others who hoped to move west, opposed any restriction. The New England and Middle Atlantic business and industrial interests were in favor, believing restriction would prevent a drain of workers away from the factories. Southern spokesmen, who were concerned about northern opposition to both slavery and the doctrine of states' rights, but who had small direct interest in the land matter, sided with the West. They hoped to gain support, in return, for opposition to high tariffs. When the Foot resolution was debated, beginning in January, 1830, the discussion broadened into an examination of the foundations of the American Union, with Daniel Webster (1782–1852) and Robert Y. Hayne (1791–1839) as the protagonists of two opposing philosophies of government.

Webster, Calhoun and Clay were the dominant figures in the Senate, and of them Webster was without doubt the best orator. Born in New Hampshire, he taught in a country school at the age of fifteen, went to Dartmouth College (where he excelled in debate, which was a competitive sport in those days), became a lawyer and by 1813 represented his native state in the House of Representatives. A few years later he moved to Massachusetts and was a representative from that state from 1823 to 1827. In his early legislative days, Webster took a restricted view of the Federal government's powers and sided with New England's shipping and mercantile interests in opposing high protective tariffs. As New England turned to manufacturing, and as the South rather than New England adopted states' rights as its standard, Webster shifted to the opposite side of these issues.

Massachusetts sent him to the Senate in 1827. As his career progressed, Webster was a capable secretary of state and several times a candidate, or would-be candidate for the presidency. He also built a reputation as a formidable lawyer in cases involving the interpretation of the Constitution. In appearance, Webster was impressive. Although he was under six feet in height, his broad shoulders, massive head and black eyes that someone said burned "as anthracite," made him seem even taller. He was called Olympian and godlike. Yet with so much in his favor, Webster never reached the summit he might have. He was too interested in his own well-being, he accepted fees and loans from persons and institutions who wanted to make use of his influence, and he liked the luxuries of life too much.

Hayne never attained Webster's public eminence, but he was a worthy debating opponent who stated well and firmly the position of the South. Hayne was born in South Carolina, and was elected to the Senate in 1823, where he served until 1832. He was the South's voice against high tariffs. Hayne also served as governor of South Carolina from 1832 to 1834, thus being the chief executive of that state when the crisis over nullification came to a head. When he debated Webster, Hayne was a slender, handsome, rather boyish-looking man who was at ease in his role.

The debate began on January 19, 1830, when Hayne spoke against the Foot resolution, invoking the rights of the states and assailing Federal intervention. He asserted that "the very life of our system is the independence of the states and . . . there is no evil more to be deprecated than the consolidation of this government." Webster replied the next day, attacking those who disparaged the Union. Both men spoke twice more, with the debate having left specific issues far behind. The basic nature of the Constitution and of the Union was the real issue. Hayne defined and defended the doctrine of state sovereignty and argued for the right of a state to nullify Federal laws. On January 26, in what became known as Webster's Second Reply, the statesman from Massachusetts argued that it was "the people's Constitution," and that it and the Federal government were supreme over the people. States were not sovereign. Webster closed one of the great orations in the country's history with these words:

When my eyes shall be turned to behold for the last time the sun in heaven, may I not see him shining on the broken and dishonored fragments of a once glorious Union; on States dissevered, discordant, belligerent; on a land rent with civil feuds, or drenched, it may be, in fraternal blood! Let their last feeble and lingering glance rather behold

the gorgeous ensign of the republic, now known and honored throughout the earth, still full high advanced, its arms and trophies streaming
in their original lustre, not a stripe erased or polluted, not a single star
obscured, bearing for its motto, no such miserable interrogatory as
'What is all this worth?' nor those words of delusion and folly, 'Liberty
first and Union afterwards'; but everywhere, spread all over in
characters of living light, blazing in all its ample folds, as they float over
the sea and over the land, and in every wind under the whole heavens,
that other sentiment, dear to every true American heart,—Liberty *and*
Union, now and forever, one and inseparable!

The specific act that set in motion the events of the nullification
crisis of 1832 was the Tariff of 1828, known to its enemies as the "tariff
of abominations." The South was anti-tariff in practice and in
principle, and this latest bill, which increased the rates on imported
goods and materials the South had to buy, seemed the last straw.

The state legislatures of South Carolina, Georgia, Mississippi and
Virginia reacted by passing resolutions that called the tariff both
unfair and unconstitutional. South Carolina's resolution, in December, 1828, was accompanied by an "Exposition and Protest," issued
anonymously but known to be the work of Vice-President Calhoun. It
attacked the tariff as an unfair tax on the South, but its importance
lay in Calhoun's presentation of the theory of states' rights, including
the right of one state to nullify an act of Congress. The Federal
government, he said, was one of strictly limited powers, an agreement
among the states. Calhoun argued that any state had the right to
"interpose" its rights and power to prevent a national law from
operating within its boundaries until and unless three-fourths of the
states gave force to the law by amending the Constitution.

Thus John C. Calhoun (1782–1850) completed his journey from
strong nationalist to leading exponent of states' rights. Born on a farm
in South Carolina, and always at heart a farmer, he went to Yale
College and then studied law. By 1811 he was a member of the House
of Representatives where he was one of the foremost "War Hawks,"
urging war with Great Britain. In this period he advocated internal

improvements at Federal government expense, and supported the protective tariff of 1816. After serving as secretary of war under President James Monroe, he was elected vice-president in 1824 and re-elected in 1828.

Calhoun's loyalties and political beliefs changed as the North industrialized while the South became more and more wedded to a cotton-growing economy based on slavery. The more rapid growth of the North threatened to end the domination of the government which the South had enjoyed—at least in Congress—for many years. Calhoun found himself the voice for thousands of southerners who felt they were being overwhelmed by events and by the government in Washington, and who saw their salvation in the doctrine of states' rights. In 1832, having broken with Jackson and seeking a better position from which to defend the South, Calhoun resigned the vice-presidency so that his home state could send him to the Senate.

Calhoun never received the popular acclaim that was given Jackson or Webster, but he was greatly admired, almost revered, in the South. Like Jackson, he was tall (six feet, two inches) and gaunt. His stiff gray hair and fierce black eyes gave him a formidable appearance, which was not helped by his harsh speaking voice. He was, as one foreign visitor wrote, "a cast iron man."

His philosophy was stated in two books published after his death. In them he carried his theories of restricted Federal government even further, yet here as elsewhere Calhoun wanted to preserve the Union. Believing that the greatest danger lay in the power of a numerical majority over a minority, Calhoun proposed the idea of a "concurrent" majority. The majority and minority groups would each have veto power over the other, perhaps through a scheme of two executive officers. Accommodation would then be worked out between the opposing groups.

Calhoun and Jackson were on opposite sides of the conflict between the South and the government in Washington, and Jackson made it clear he would have nothing to do with nullification. The laws

of the United States must be obeyed. The first public showdown
between Jackson and Calhoun occurred at a Jefferson Day dinner in
Washington in April, 1830. When called on for a toast, Jackson in a
few blunt words stated his position: "Our Federal Union, it must be
preserved." Calhoun, apparently somewhat taken aback, replied:
"The Union—next to our liberty most dear."

Later that year, in his annual message to Congress, Jackson
defended the constitutionality of the Tariff of 1828 and the idea of
protection in general. Although a new tariff act in 1832 removed
many of the items in the "tariff of abominations" which had so
angered the South, South Carolina was not satisfied. A convention was
called by the legislature and met in November. It passed an ordinance
which declared the two tariff acts void in South Carolina, forbade the
collection of customs duties in the state, and asserted that the use of
force by the Federal government would be cause for secession from the
Union.

President Jackson reacted in the only way he knew. First, he
reinforced two forts in South Carolina and put Major General
Winfield Scott in command of military forces in the state. Then, on
December 10, 1832, he issued a proclamation to the people of South
Carolina in which he warned:

> I consider, then, the power to annul a law of the United States, assumed
> by one state, incompatible with the existence of the Union, contradicted
> expressly by the letter of the Constitution, unauthorized by its spirit,
> inconsistent with every principle on which it was founded, and
> destructive of the great object for which it was formed. . . .

Going a step further, the president took issue with Calhoun's theory of
the American government:

> The Constitution of the United States, then, forms a *government,* not a
> league; and whether it be formed by compact between the states or in
> any other manner, its character is the same. It is a government in which
> all the people are represented, which operates directly on the people

individually, not upon the States; they retained all the power they did not grant. But each State, having expressly parted with so many powers as to constitute, jointly with the other States, a single nation, can not, from that period, possess any right to secede, because such secession does not break a league, but destroys the unity of a nation; and any injury to that unity is not only a breach which would result from the contravention of a compact, but it is an offense against the whole Union . . . .

Finally, Jackson in January, 1833, asked Congress to pass a Force Bill which would give the president power to enforce the tariff law by the use of the military if necessary. Calhoun led a fight against the bill, but it passed and was signed by Jackson on March 2. Meanwhile, Jackson had urged Congress to revise the tariff downward to appease the South, and Henry Clay sponsored such a measure which became law the same day as the Force Bill. By its terms, custom duties would be reduced over ten years to a level equal to about 20 per cent of the rates in the hated "tariff of abominations." After this action, South Carolina suspended its ordinance of nullification, but to show its mood adopted another ordinance declaring the Force Bill null and void. No one pressed the issue further and both sides were, for the time being, satisfied.

The other major crisis of Jackson's first term involved the banking system of the country and, specifically, the Second Bank of the United States. The Bank was chartered by act of Congress in 1816 for a term of twenty years, and it was the Federal government's only official connection with the banking world. The Bank was capitalized at $35,000,000, of which a fifth was subscribed by the government. The president appointed five of the twenty-five directors and the share-holders elected the rest. In addition, the government received $1,500,000 from the Bank for the charter privilege. The Bank could lend money, issue notes which the government would accept in payment of taxes, act as a depository for government funds and a disbursing agent for its expenses. Despite its close relationship with the government, the Bank was a profit-making institution, controlled by its shareholders and directors.

Otherwise, the nation's banking system consisted of a growing number of banks under state regulation. Laws varied greatly from state to state, there was little effective regulation, and many men who set themselves up as bankers had small understanding of their profession. Between 1829 and 1837 the number of banks increased from 329 to 788, and most of the increase was in the West. The banks issued notes and granted loans with insufficient specie (coined money) in many cases to back them up. Notes in circulation increased in that same period from $48,000,000 to $149,000,000, and loans from $137,000,000 to $525,000,000. A rapidly expanding nation needed money to finance the building of factories and other facilities and the purchase of public land in the West, but speculation for quick profits lured bankers and their customers into overextending the system.

By contrast, the Bank of the United States, with headquarters in Philadelphia, was sound and solvent and a strong force against inflation. Unfortunately, the bank became involved in politics and in a struggle between opposing views of the economic system. Except for New York banking interests which were jealous of the Bank's power and prestige, conservative business and financial interests favored the Bank. Western and southern bankers, on the other hand, hated it because its operations restrained their inflationary tendencies. The Bank did this by presenting, as fast as received, these state banks' notes for redemption in specie. Advocates of "hard money," including working people who sometimes were paid with paper currency of fluctuating value, approved the high standards of the Bank. Those who wanted cheap money and easy credit for expansion and speculation disliked the Bank. As time went on, a substantial part of the Bank's stock was owned abroad and this was an argument against it in the eyes of some Americans. In sum, the Bank in 1832 was efficient and had many good points, but it had too much uncontrolled power for its special relationship to the government.

In addition, the Bank's president, the talented Nicholas Biddle (1786–1844), became a controversial figure. Biddle came from a

wealthy Philadelphia family. He graduated from Princeton at the age
of fifteen, wrote an account of the Lewis and Clark expedition of
1803–1806 from the Mississippi River to the Pacific coast, and for a
while was editor of the *Port Folio*, a literary magazine. Appointed a
director of the Bank in 1819, he became its president in 1823. He
expanded its operations and curried favor with politicians and editors
by lending them money, or, as in the case of Daniel Webster, paying
him an annual retainer as counsel.

Supporters of the Bank, with Henry Clay in the forefront,
decided that it would be better to press for a new charter in 1832,
rather than wait until nearer 1836 when the charter expired. Clay
mistakenly thought Jackson would be hurt in the forthcoming
presidential election if he opposed the Bank, and Clay hoped to be his
opponent in the race. The bill passed Congress in July and, accepting
Clay's challenge, Jackson vetoed it. In his annual message in 1829,
Jackson had questioned the constitutionality of the Bank and spoke in
favor of a more restricted institution wholly owned by the government.
In his veto message he went further in attacking the power wielded by
such an institution under private control. In general, though, Jackson
ignored the economic arguments on both sides and concentrated on an
appeal to "the humble members of society" against "the rich and
powerful." The president lost some support in New York and New
England by his veto, but events supported his view that the people
were behind him.

Jackson was not content with his victory and in 1833 pressed his
assault on the Bank. He resolved to stop using the Bank as the sole
depository of government funds. According to the law, funds could be
deposited elsewhere only if the secretary of the treasury so ordered,
and the secretary was required to give Congress his reasons. To his
surprise, Jackson found his treasury department head, Louis McLane
(1786–1857), unwilling to go along with the scheme. He transferred
McLane to the position of secretary of state, but he had no better luck
with McLane's successor, William J. Duane (1780–1865), whom he

then simply dismissed. Finally, by shifting Roger B. Taney from the attorney generalship to the treasury, Jackson found a supporter. Taney announced in September, 1833, that no more funds would be deposited in the Bank and that government money on deposit would be drawn on to pay bills until exhausted. Federal funds were to be deposited in selected state banks and by the end of 1833, twenty-three such banks had been favored. Opponents dubbed them "pet banks."

Neither Congress nor Nicholas Biddle accepted this action without protest. The Senate demanded that Jackson submit a paper he had read to his cabinet outlining his reasons for the move. Jackson refused on the grounds of executive privilege, contending that the legislature had no authority to require any communication from the president. Biddle proceeded to call in loans and to greatly restrict the credit granted by the Bank. Since he had reason to fear what Jackson might do next, and since no more government deposits were forthcoming, Biddle had some justification for reducing the Bank's activities. However, he carried his policy into the spring of 1834 and by then it was causing panic even among supporters and fellow bankers. Jackson refused to back down and eventually the situation improved when Biddle eased up on credit.

Between the Bank veto and the removal of deposits, Jackson won a most satisfying victory in the presidential election of 1832. The campaign was the first for which candidates were nominated at national conventions, and the first in which a third party played a role. The Democrats enthusiastically renominated their hero, Jackson. Martin Van Buren of New York, Jackson's chief adviser and heir apparent, was named for vice-president. The National Republican convention nominated Henry Clay for president and John Sergeant of New York for vice-president. Clay was a nationalist who believed in a strong Federal government. He was one of the peace commissioners who negotiated the end of the War of 1812, and was a leading figure in working out the Missouri Compromise of 1820. After serving as secretary of state under John Quincy Adams, Clay returned to the Senate where he led the National Republicans.

The new third party grew out of a wave of suspicion and hatred of the Free and Accepted Masons, a secret fraternal order that traced its history back to the Middle Ages and whose first lodge in America was established in 1730. Many prominent Americans, including George Washington, Thomas Jefferson and Andrew Jackson, were Masons, but some people considered it a snobbish order and suspected it of wielding secret influence within the government. An anti-Masonic party was formed after the mysterious disappearance in 1826 of William Morgan (1774?–1826?) in New York State. Morgan was a Mason who had made it known that he was going to write an exposé of the order. Official inquiries and trials threw no light on what had happened to Morgan, but did disclose that almost all the officeholders in New York were Masons. By 1827 the Anti-Masonic party was strong enough to elect fifteen members of the state legislature from western New York. At its 1832 convention, the party nominated for president William Wirt (1772–1834) of Maryland. Wirt was a distinguished lawyer who had been the government's chief prosecutor at Aaron Burr's 1807 treason trial, and attorney general of the United States from 1817 to 1829.

Jackson stood for a number of causes that appealed to different groups and sections, but his personal campaign was waged against the Bank—that "monster," as he called it. Although he won a smaller share of the popular vote than in 1828, 687,000 to 530,000 for Clay, he achieved a larger majority in the Electoral College, 16 of the 24 states and 219 votes to 49. Wirt carried only Vermont with 7 votes, while South Carolina cast its 11 votes for a favorite son.

3 Jackson, Van Buren and Depression

In HIS second term—from 1833 to 1837—Jackson faced no major issues, but he was active and aggressive. Nor were his enemies idle in attempts to harass him.

In December, 1833, after Jackson refused the Senate's request for the paper he had read to his cabinet about ceasing to deposit funds in the Bank, Henry Clay introduced two resolutions of censure. One declared that the president had no authority to remove William J. Duane as secretary of the treasury when Duane refused to transfer deposits to state banks. The other declared that the reasons given by the administration for its action on deposits were "unsatisfactory and insufficient."

After a three months' debate, in which Webster and Calhoun sided with Clay, the resolutions were approved. Jackson protested the censuring resolutions and asked that his protest be entered in the Senate's records. This the Senate refused to do. The Senate also refused to confirm Jackson's appointment of Taney as secretary of the treasury. In spite of these setbacks, Jackson's hold on the voters was demonstrated in the midterm elections of 1834. The Democrats increased their margin in the House to 145 to 98, and took control of the Senate by a narrow margin. In January, 1837, the Democratic majority in the Senate literally expunged the offending resolutions, drawing black lines around them in the Senate journal.

When Chief Justice John Marshall died in 1835, after serving as head of the Supreme Court ever since President John Adams appointed him early in 1801, Jackson had an opportunity to name a new chief justice whose views on government and the Constitution were more in accord with his. He named Roger B. Taney (1777–1864), a member of a wealthy, slave-holding, tobacco-growing Maryland family. Taney entered politics as a Federalist, but changed his views and supported Jackson from 1824 on. Taney was the chief author of Jackson's veto message on the rechartering of the Bank. The Senate in 1835 declined to confirm Taney as an associate justice of the Supreme Court. The following year, however, with the number of Democrats increased, Taney was confirmed as chief justice, a post which he held for twenty-eight years.

Where Marshall had led the Court in supporting the rights of private property and in interpreting the Constitution to give wide power to the Federal government, Taney headed a court—now dominated by appointments by a Democratic president—that took a more restricted view of both matters. In the realm of property rights and contracts, the Taney court's 1837 decision in the Charles River Bridge case considerably altered previous court opinions. Years earlier the state of Massachusetts had granted a company a charter to build a toll bridge over the Charles River. Now, the company sued the state when a charter was granted to another company to build a new bridge nearby that would be toll-free as soon as its construction costs were recovered. The Court ruled that the charter contained no implied powers that gave the original company a monopoly, and it thus constricted the judicial view of contracts compared with the Marshall court.

That same year, in a case known as *City of New York* v. *Miln*, Taney and the court declared, in effect, that a single state could make laws that concerned interstate commerce so long as Congress had not legislated in the same matter. Taney's predecessor had said that only Congress could legislate in this field. Another decision expanded the power of states to act for the public welfare; another, while recognizing the usefulness of the corporate form of business organization, refused to agree that a corporation had the same status as a citizen.

Jackson's personality and methods helped settle the French Spoliation Claims in 1836. France in 1831 agreed to pay the United States 25,000,000 francs, and the United States agreed to pay France 1,500,000 to settle claims growing out of attacks on each other's merchant ships during the Napoleonic Wars. When France was slow in making payment, Jackson recommended to Congress that the United States take reprisals on French property. The French voted an appropriation in the spring of 1835, on condition that Jackson apologize for the language he had used. Jackson refused, insisting he would never allow a foreign government to "dictate" his language. The president, in January, 1836, again threatened reprisals but at the same time offered conciliation. Great Britain stepped in to mediate the quarrel, and by May France paid four of the six installments.

Jackson's actions with regard to banking, currency and public finance did not end with his victory over the Bank of the United States. He and his supporters pushed a "hard money" policy. The valuation of gold was increased so that those who mined gold would find it more profitable to have it coined. Positive results showed in the growth in the amount of specie in the country: $30,000,000 in the fall of 1833 and $73,000,000 by December, 1836. Steps were also taken to cut down on the amount of paper currency put out by banks. During this period government revenues, chiefly from customs duties and the sale of public lands, greatly exceeded expenses. In 1836, receipts from public-land sales were larger than customs duties for the first and only time. The national debt was entirely paid off by January, 1835, but never again was the nation free of debt. Surplus funds became such an embarrassment to the Federal government that in 1837, under a plan proposed by Clay, $28,000,000 was distributed to the states.

As a further step to augment his hard money policy, Jackson, in July, 1836, issued a Specie Circular which provided that after August 15, only gold and silver coins would be accepted in payment for public lands. Congress tried to kill the plan, but Jackson vetoed the bill. Two years later, the Specie Circular was repealed by a joint resolution of Congress. Some of the administration's actions helped hold down inflation, but others did not, while still other factors were beyond its control.

The use and disposal of the millions of acres of public land west of the Alleghenies posed problems beyond those related to public finance. Jackson and the Democrats favored a policy that made land available easily and cheaply. This contradicted the hard money policy because it called for cheaper money and expansion of credit so that those with little or no savings could take up enough acreage for a self-sufficient farm. In addition, the more liberal the policy, the more it encouraged speculators to buy up large tracts and hold them until they rose in value. The common people—farmers, mechanics and laborers—favored the Jacksonian policy. Manufacturing interests wanted a stricter policy so that the labor supply would not be decreased, thereby raising wages. Not nearly as many urban workers went west to buy public lands as was once supposed. Most of those who went west to farm were already farmers, or sons of farmers seeking their own homesteads, or, increasingly, emigrants from Europe.

Many settlers did not wait for the government to put a tract of land on sale but simply moved in and "squatted" on the land. These squatters formed "claim associations" for mutual protection when the land was officially opened to purchase. They respected each others' claims, and threatened or even used force on any outsiders who tried to buy land already occupied. As early as 1830, Congress passed a pre-emption act that allowed settlers who had cultivated land of the public domain in 1829 to buy up to 160 acres at $1.25 an acre. The Pre-Emption Act of 1841 made it permanent policy to recognize settlement before purchase, and to consider settlement of the land by pioneers more important than the revenue that might be obtained from land sales. Five years later Andrew Johnson, a future president, introduced the first bill to give land free to pioneer farmers, but it did not become law. Sales of public lands were increasing steadily. In 1834, 4,500,000 acres were sold; the next year the figure went over 12,000,000; and in 1836 topped 20,000,000. The government set up land offices to handle the sale and they were so busy that the expression "doing a land office business" entered the language.

On March 4, 1837, Andrew Jackson's second term in the presidency came to an end. No president until then left so strong a mark on the office. He expanded presidential power, making it less dependent on either the cabinet or Congress. He saw himself as a direct representative of the people who should look out for their interests both at home and abroad. Jackson's approach to his duties and his personal style were clear in his use of the presidential veto. The six earlier presidents together vetoed only nine bills passed by Congress, and primarily on the grounds that they thought a bill unconstitutional. Jackson vetoed twelve bills and used the power simply because he disagreed with what Congress wanted to do.

Jackson's faults as well as his virtues were readily apparent. His approach to public matters was too personal, based more on instinct than reflection. He made some bad choices of men to fill important positions, and his understanding of basic social and economic problems was slight. Yet he became a symbol of the times and the ideal of many Americans. One foreign visitor, Alexis de Tocqueville, a liberal politician and writer from France, saw Jackson as "a man of violent temper and mediocre talent." Another visitor, Harriet Martineau, an English commentator on public affairs, gave a more rounded appraisal:

> If ever there was a possibility of a president marking his age, for good or for evil, it would have been done during Jackson's administration. He is a man made to impress a very distinct idea of himself on all minds. He has great personal courage, much sagacity, though frequently impaired by the strength of his prejudices, violent passions, an indomitable will, and that devotion to public affairs in which no president has ever failed.

The man the Democrats nominated for president in 1836—with the blessing of Old Hickory—was a complete contrast to the retiring hero. Martin Van Buren (1782–1862) was born in Kinderhook, New York, where his father was both a farmer and a tavern-keeper. Van Buren studied law and became a lawyer, but his lifelong occupation was that of politician and officeholder. He began his career working for the election of Thomas Jefferson in 1800, and in 1821 New York State sent him to the Senate. He served until 1828 when he was elected governor of the state, a post he resigned the next year to become Jackson's secretary of state. During these years Van Buren was the recognized leader among a group of astute politicians who built up the Democratic party in New York. Jackson nominated him in 1831 to be minister to Great Britain, but Vice-President Calhoun cast the deciding vote against confirming the nomination. By then, though, Van Buren's tact, diplomacy and political astuteness had made him Jackson's political heir.

Van Buren's personality and methods led his enemies to make fun of him and to underestimate his abilities. He was considered slick in his tactics and over-fussy about his personal appearance. He was short, with a round head, and as he grew older he grew bald and a bit fat. Van Buren sported muttonchop whiskers, which his opponents claimed he perfumed, and he was also said to wear corsets. He was dubbed "Little Van," "The Red Fox of Kinderhook" and "The Little Magician." Van Buren was an honest man, somewhat deliberate in reaching decisions.

Opposing the Democrats were the Whigs, a party that formally adopted the name in 1834. The Whig party was made up of the National Republicans, of which Clay was still the leader, the followers of Calhoun and states' rights people in general, and various others who disagreed with Jackson's policies. The Whig party was conservative and business-oriented, with little appeal to western farmers.

The Whigs were not unified enough in 1836 to present a single candidate. Instead they supported three men from different sections of the country, hoping thereby to split up the Electoral College votes so that no one would get a majority and the House, where they might prevail, would have to choose the next president. In the North, Daniel Webster was the Whig standard bearer. The candidate of the South and the Southwest was Hugh L. White (1773–1840) who was born in North Carolina but moved to Tennessee, which he represented in the Senate from 1825 to 1840. White supported Jackson until 1835 when he fell out with him over currency policy. The third candidate, who ran on the Anti-Masonic party ticket also, was William Henry Harrison (1773–1841). Born in Virginia, he carved out careers in the army and in the Old Northwest, being appointed the first governor of Indiana Territory in 1801. He negotiated a number of treaties with Indian tribes by which they gave up large tracts to the United States and in November, 1811, he won a close victory over the Indians in the Battle of Tippecanoe. During the War of 1812, Harrison was one of the few successful American generals, commanding the forces that won the Battle of the Thames in October, 1813. He served as senator from Ohio from 1825 to 1828.

There was little discussion of issues in the campaign. Van Buren clearly stood for the policies of the previous eight years. His opponents were against those policies and voters chose sides mostly on a pro- or anti-Jackson basis. Van Buren received 761,549 votes, more than the 736,250 received by all his opponents. Harrison was by far the best vote-getter among the Whigs, with 549,567. In the Electoral College, Van Buren, carrying 15 of the 26 states, received 170 votes; Harrison, 73; White, 26; Webster, 14; and South Carolina again gave its votes to a favorite son. For the first and only time, no vice-presidential candidate received a majority of the electoral votes so the Senate had to choose, electing Richard M. Johnson (1781–1850) of Kentucky, 33 to 16.

On March 4, 1837, Martin Van Buren became president, the first president born after the Declaration of Independence, the first from New York State and the first of Dutch descent. His inaugural address repeated Jacksonian themes, but he aroused the antislavery forces by opposing abolition in the District of Columbia unless the southern states agreed.

The Van Buren administration was plagued by the Panic of 1837 and its aftermath. The closing of the Second Bank of the United States removed the only restraining influence on the banking system. The deposit of Federal funds in the pet banks, and the distribution of surplus funds to the states, created more credit and more inflation. The Specie Circular drained gold and silver to the West, made money tight in the East, and created more doubts about the soundness of the banking system. Speculation in land became a mania and prices went up unrealistically. The states, especially in the West and South, spent large sums on internal improvements, all based on borrowed money. A financial crisis in England helped trigger the panic when British banks demanded payment of debts owed them by United States firms.

The price of cotton dropped sharply. In May, after depositors withdrew $1,000,000 in gold and silver, the New York banks stopped paying out specie and the rest of the banks in the country followed suit. Many states ceased paying interest on their debts and four repudiated in whole or part the debts themselves. Nicholas Biddle's United States Bank of Pennsylvania, successor to the Bank of the United States, suspended payments in 1839 and failed completely in 1841. Crop failures in 1835 and 1837 added to the trouble, leaving farmers unable to meet financial obligations. The depression which followed the panic was a long one, lasting until 1843. Real-estate values fell, as did stock and commodity prices. Unemployment was widespread and in New York a mob invaded flour warehouses and carted away as much as possible.

Van Buren called a special session of Congress to meet in September, 1837, but he was more concerned that it deal with the government's own financial problems, which were compounded by falling revenue and the suspension of specie payment by the pet banks, than with the panic as such. In his message to the session the president took a narrow view of the government's responsibility for doing anything about a depression. He asserted that

> . . . the less government interferes with private pursuits the better for the general prosperity. It is not its legitimate object to make men rich or to repair by direct grants of money or legislation in favor of particular pursuits, losses not incurred in the public service. This would be substantially to use the property of some for the benefit of others.

The major proposal in Van Buren's message was to establish an Independent Treasury System, under which the government would hold its own funds and make its own disbursements. The Whigs and other conservatives twice defeated such a bill, in 1837 and 1838, although Calhoun and his followers favored it. In 1840 Van Buren was finally able to get his plan approved. Subtreasuries were set up in seven cities to handle government funds, and the law required that by June 30, 1843, all payments to and disbursements by the government should be in hard money. The Whigs, however, back in control of Congress in 1841, repealed the Independent Treasury Act so that until 1846 the handling of money was left to the secretary of the treasury, who once more relied on the state banks.

As well as having difficulties at home, the Van Buren administration was involved in trouble with Canada in two incidents, one known as the *Caroline* Affair and the other the "Aroostook War." The *Caroline* incident began when a revolt broke out in Canada in 1837 aimed at securing a more democratic system of government. The leader was William Lyon Mackenzie (1795–1861), a journalist born in Scotland. He failed in an attempt to seize Toronto, fled to the United States and set up a government on Navy Island in the Niagara River. The United States imprisoned him for eighteen months for violation of neutrality laws. Considerable sentiment existed in the United States in favor of the insurgents, and in the Niagara River a ship, the *Caroline*, owned by American citizens, was used to smuggle men and supplies into Canada. On December 29, 1837, a group of loyal Canadians and

British seized the ship, set it afire and let it drift toward the falls. One American was killed in the foray and anger against Canada grew so intense that troops under General Scott were moved to the scene to prevent violence. Nearly three years later, in November, 1840, a former Canadian deputy sheriff, Alexander McLeod, while in Buffalo, New York, boasted that he had killed the American, Amos Durfee, who had died in the attack on the *Caroline*. After being held for eleven months he was tried and acquitted. The *Caroline* Affair ended there, but bad feeling remained on both sides.

The "Aroostook War" was a bloodless war, but violence almost broke out before cooler heads prevailed. The boundary between Maine and New Brunswick had never been settled, and the dispute reached a climax in 1838–39. New Brunswick loggers entered the area, centered on the Aroostook River Valley, in which Maine farmers were also interested. Maine raised a force to eject the lumbermen but the latter surprised the American posse and jailed fifty of them. Maine retaliated by seizing a Canadian warden of the territory, and New Brunswick asked for British troops. Van Buren again made use of General Scott, sending him to the region more to prevent further trouble than to enforce American claims. The general negotiated a truce.

Twelve years of Jacksonian democracy in the White House ended with the expiration of Van Buren's term in 1841, but the Jacksonian era was not over. In fact, the Democrats, with their Jacksonian foundation, dominated national politics until the Civil War. In the thirty-two years from Jackson's first election to that of Abraham Lincoln, the Democrats won six of the eight presidential elections and put five Democrats in the White House. The two Whig candidates elected were both military heroes, short on political experience. Jacksonian democracy was the heir to the Jeffersonian tradition of trust in the common person and opposition to vested interests, but in the twenty years between Jefferson's departure from the White House and Jackson's entry, the nation changed its way of life. The population spread over a larger area while the steady growth of manufacturing and better transportation facilities altered the economic life of the nation.

The Jacksonians were successful, at least in part, because they recognized and accepted these changes. The Democrats appealed to the working people and farmers, but in an era of expanding capitalism, did not oppose capitalism and industrialism as such. They were against only those persons already in positions of economic power who tried to keep others from enjoying the benefits of individualistic capitalism. Jackson's basic position regarding government and business was well stated in his 1832 message in which he vetoed the rechartering of the Bank of the United States:

> It is to be regretted that the rich and the powerful too often bend the acts of government to their selfish purposes. Distinctions in society will always exist under every just government. Equality of talents, of education, or of wealth can not be produced by human institutions. In the full enjoyment of the gifts of Heaven and the fruits of superior industry, economy, and virtue, every man is equally entitled to protection by law; but when the laws undertake to add to these natural and just advantages artificial distinctions, to grant titles, gratuities, and exclusive privileges, to make the rich richer and the potent more powerful, the humble members of society—the farmers, mechanics, and laborers—who have neither the time nor the means of securing like favors to themselves, have a right to complain of the injustices of their government.

The Jacksonians did not object to capitalism; what they said they wanted to do was to give every person a chance to become a capitalist. It was, as one writer noted, the "democracy of expectant capitalists."

4 Harrison, Tyler and Polk

THE CAMPAIGN for the presidency in 1840 was something new in American politics. It started calmly enough with the Democrats unanimously renominating Van Buren. When the Whigs met, Clay was the leading contender, but he faced strong opposition because of his poor showing in 1832. Many Whigs favored nominating a military hero, either Scott or Harrison. Harrison won, partly because of the strong vote-getting ability he had shown in the 1836 election. For vice-president, the Whigs named John Tyler of Virginia, who had been a Democrat until he broke with Jackson. The Whigs hoped Tyler would attract votes from southerners who would not support a ticket consisting of northern Whigs only.

The Anti-Masonic party was now blended into the Whig party, and its leader was on his way to becoming the boss of the Whig machine. He was Thurlow Weed (1797–1882), a New York State journalist and political leader, who fought the Albany Regency of Van Buren and his group. Genial but unscrupulous, he edited an influential paper, the Albany *Evening Journal*. In 1840, for the first time, an antislavery ticket was in the contest. The small Liberty Party, formed by delegates from six states, nominated James G. Birney of Kentucky. The slavery issue also appeared in a major party platform for the first time when the Democrats declared that Congress had no power to interfere with that institution in the slave states.

To the dismay of the Democrats, the campaign turned into a

popularity contest in which the Whigs far outdid the Democrats in the use of irrelevant issues and appeals to emotions. A Democratic paper jibed at the Whigs that "upon condition of his receiving a pension of $2,000 and a barrel of cider, General Harrison would no doubt consent to withdraw his pretensions, and spend his days in a log cabin on the banks of the Ohio." In fact, Harrison came from an aristocratic Virginia family and his house in Ohio was large and comfortable. The Whigs cleverly turned the jibe against the Democrats. They made placards showing Harrison at the door of a log cabin, welcoming visitors to his humble home. Coonskins hung on the wall and a cider barrel was handy. Miniature log cabins were mounted on wagons and featured in parades and rallies. Cider, some hard and possibly spiked with whiskey, flowed freely.

The Whigs also made the most of Harrison's war record with the cry of "Tippecanoe and Tyler Too," while they derided Van Buren as "Martin Van Ruin," and chanted the slogan, "Van, Van is a used up man." They charged that Van Buren drank large amounts of champagne at the taxpayers' expense, and also bought finger bowls "in which to wash his pretty, tapering, soft, white lily-fingers, after dining on fricandeau de veau and omelette soufflé." Neither side said much about economic and political problems, and Van Buren bore the burden of the panic and depression of his first term.

The Whig tactics were effective. Nearly 2,500,000 votes were cast, many more than in any previous election. Harrison received 1,275,017 votes to Van Buren's 1,128,702 (366,000 more than he won in 1836), but in the Electoral College the margin for Harrison was much greater. He carried 19 of the 26 states with 234 electoral votes to 60, and the Whigs also won control of both houses of Congress. Birney got only 7,000 votes.

Even before his inauguration on March 4, 1841, Harrison was caught up in the internal differences of the Whigs. Webster was named secretary of state, a post which he wanted as a steppingstone to the presidency. Clay, still ambitious to be chief executive, refused a cabinet position. He hoped to control the administration from his seat in the Senate. Meanwhile, with a turnover in party control of the governmental machinery, the old and infirm president was besieged every day with office-seekers. Before the end of March, Harrison caught a cold which developed into pneumonia and exactly one month after he took office he was dead.

John Tyler (1790–1862) was the first vice-president to succeed to the presidency and, at fifty-one, was the youngest man in the office. Since no precedent existed, the question arose as to whether Tyler was merely the acting president. Tyler believed he had taken over the office, not just the duties, and was not challenged. He was a lawyer who entered the political scene as a Jeffersonian in the House in 1817. From 1825 to 1827 he was governor of Virginia and then served in the Senate until 1836. A supporter of states' rights, Tyler nevertheless backed Jackson in 1828 and 1832 because he seemed the least objectionable candidate. He condemned Jackson, however, for his actions in Florida. He also voted against the Missouri Compromise in 1820. Jackson's Force Bill during the nullification crisis and his fiscal policies drove Tyler out of the Democratic party. He was an honest, hard-working man with a mind of his own; he was mild-mannered, genial and well-liked in Virginia. However, not a true Whig, out of sympathy with the northern, conservative wing, and a man the Whigs never intended to be president, Tyler was doomed to head an administration full of bickering and frustration. Clay and Webster both wanted to control him and to shape the Whig party in their interests.

The most important domestic issues during the Tyler administration were the continuing battle over fiscal policy, and the question of whether to reestablish a bank like the one refused a new charter in 1832. Under Clay's leadership, the Whigs proposed setting up a financial institution to be called the Fiscal Bank of the United States. In effect a revival of the Bank of the United States, the Fiscal Bank was to be capitalized at $30,000,000 and would be permitted to establish branches in any state unless the state legislature objected. Tyler vetoed the bill in August, 1841, as unconstitutional and because it went against his states' rights beliefs. A second bill was prepared to meet Tyler's objections and it was understood he would approve it, but he vetoed it also. All members of the cabinet except Webster resigned, and for the rest of the administration no practical relations existed between Tyler and the Whigs.

Tyler fought also with Congress over the tariff. In July, 1842, tariff rates reached the low point specified by the Compromise Tariff of 1833. The government debt, however, had increased in six years from nothing to $13,500,000, and more revenue from customs duties was needed. Twice in 1842 Congress passed tariff bills but Tyler vetoed them because they contained a provision for distributing surplus revenue to the states. A bill was finally passed without this provision, restoring tariff rates to about where they had been in 1832. Among Tyler's other troubles was the action of Congress, on the very last day of his term, of overriding a presidential veto, the first time this ever happened.

Soon after he became secretary of state, Webster took the initiative in negotiations with Great Britain over a number of matters, and he and Baron Ashburton, who was sent to Washington in the spring of 1842, began amicably working out their problems. The Webster-Ashburton Treaty brought a final settlement of the Maine-New Brunswick boundary that had caused the "Aroostook War," and confirmed boundary lines between Canada and New York and Vermont. The British also agreed on a boundary from Lake Superior westward to Lake of the Woods that, it turned out later, gave the United States the rich Mesabi iron deposits. The two nations agreed to cooperate in suppressing the African slave trade and Ashburton separately apologized for the *Caroline* Affair, thereby disposing of it once and for all. Webster resigned from the cabinet in 1843 and in 1845 once more entered the Senate.

When the time arrived for the presidential election of 1844, Tyler badly wanted to be elected in his own right. He tried to establish a new party by appointing his supporters to government positions, and a group of Tyler Democrats nominated him. Tyler soon saw, however, that he had no chance and withdrew—the first president not to stand for a second term. Once again the Whigs chose Clay and he ran for the last time. The Liberty party renominated James G. Birney on a platform concerned entirely with slavery. The Democratic convention was held in Baltimore, and was the first ever reported by telegraph since the original line, new that year, connected Baltimore and Washington. Van Buren had the most votes at first, but not enough to be nominated against southern opposition. After nine ballots, the convention chose the first "dark horse" in American politics, James K. Polk (1795–1849) of Tennessee who had the support of Andrew Jackson, but was little-known nationally. George M. Dallas (1792–1864), a native of Philadelphia, who had been a senator (1831–33) and minister to Russia (1837–39), was nominated for vice-president.

Polk was born in North Carolina, but like Old Hickory he made his career in Tennessee. He served in the House of Representatives from 1825 to 1839 and was speaker after 1835. He was elected governor of Tennessee but failed to be reelected in 1841. Polk was a slaveholder who inherited a plantation in Tennessee and later, in partnership with another man, established an 880-acre plantation in Mississippi. Of medium height with sharp dark eyes, Polk was impressive by his erect carriage and dignified manner. Not especially outgoing by nature, he trained himself as a politician to be affable to those about him.

Unlike the campaign of 1840, the 1844 race for the presidency was decided on the basis of issues that were both serious and divisive. The question as to whether independent Texas should be annexed to the Union was in the forefront, and the next issue was of the extension of slavery which annexation implied. In April, Clay announced that he was against immediate annexation. After receiving the Whig nomination, however, Clay gradually modified his stand, saying he favored annexation if it could be accomplished without war with Mexico and without alienating the free states. The more Clay said in favor of annexation, the more he pleased southern voters and drove away northern Whigs.

The Democrats were more forthright in their platform and tried to satisfy both the North and the South by linking the question of Texas with that of Oregon. Their slogan was "the reoccupation of Oregon and the reannexation of Texas at the earliest practicable period." This implied that Oregon had been abandoned, which was not true except to the extent that since 1818 the United States and Britain had agreed to joint occupation of the area. As to Texas, it had never been annexed, except that some people believed Texas belonged to the United States as part of the Louisiana Purchase of 1803. The Democratic slogan, "54° 40′ or Fight," with the figures referring to the northern boundary of Oregon, was effective in the North and West where such sentiment was strong.

The election was close. Polk received 1,337,243 votes to 1,299,068 for Clay; and 170 electoral votes to 105, carrying 15 of the 26 states. Birney received 62,300 votes, about nine times as many as four years before. This was as close as Clay was to come to the presidency. He entered the Senate again in 1849 and in 1850 spoke a phrase for which he is remembered: "I would rather be right than president." The victor, Polk, at forty-nine was the youngest president to that time. An intensely hard worker who was absent from Washington only six weeks during his four-year tenure, Polk burned himself out, would not run for a second term, and died fifteen weeks after leaving office.

Polk's administration was efficient and successful in achieving his four stated goals: reduction of the tariff; restoration of the Independent Treasury System; settlement of the Oregon boundary question; and acquisition of California. The treasury system was restored in August, 1846, by act of Congress. The tariff was reduced that same year in a measure known as the Walker Tariff. This was named for Robert J. Walker (1801–69) who had been senator from Mississippi and who in Polk's cabinet became an excellent secretary of the treasury. Much of the North opposed the Walker Tariff, but it was welcomed in the South.

Behind the agitation for annexing Texas and for taking all of Oregon was a more general sentiment for continental domination that was summed up in the phrase "manifest destiny." Manifest destiny held that God, or Providence or Nature had decreed that the white, democratic American people were to rule from coast to coast in North America. The phrase itself was first used in the July-August, 1845, issue of the *Democratic Review*, edited by John L. O'Sullivan (1813–95). He wrote that nothing should stop "the fulfilment of our manifest destiny to overspread the continent allotted by Providence for the free development of our yearly multiplying millions." Polk touched on another aspect of this feeling in his first message to Congress when he elaborated on the Monroe Doctrine by stating: "The people of this continent alone have the right to decide their own destiny." And James Gordon Bennett, in the New York *Herald*, declared that the republic "must soon embrace the whole hemisphere, from the icy wilderness of the north to the most prolific regions of the smiling and prolific south."

The eyes of expansionists roamed even beyond the continent. Southern interests wanted Cuba, and in 1848 Polk offered Spain $100,000,000 but was refused. A treaty with Colombia in 1846 gave the United States the right of transit across the Isthmus of Panama. Manifest destiny operated so effectively during Polk's term that his administration added 1,204,000 square miles to American territory, more than was added by any other president except Jefferson. But this was accomplished only after suspenseful negotiations regarding Oregon and a war for Texas and California.

5   Texas and the Mexican War

AMERICAN ADVENTURERS, planters and empire-builders had had their
eyes on Texas ever since the Louisiana Purchase carried the boundary
of the United States westward to this outpost of the waning Spanish
Empire. American settlement of Texas began in 1821 when the
Mexican government granted Moses Austin land for colonizing 200
families. He died within a few months, but his son, Stephen F. Austin,
carried out the settlement. Mexico threw off Spanish rule at this same
time and became an independent nation. President John Quincy
Adams tried to buy Texas for $1,000,000, and his successor, Andrew
Jackson, offered five times as much, but to no avail.

The number of Americans in Texas increased regularly, and so
did their dissatisfaction with Mexican rule. Most came from the
American southwest, and brought with them the slaves they needed to
continue their agricultural system. Mexico abolished slavery in 1829,
prohibited further settlement by Americans, and built up its military
forces in Texas. The American-Texans petitioned for better treatment
but when Austin carried their grievances to Mexico City he was seized
and imprisoned for eight months. The Mexicans finally agreed to
allow colonization to resume, and settlers continued to move in so that
by the end of 1835 about 30,000 American-Texans far outnumbered
the 3,500 Mexicans.

Armed Mexicans and Texans clashed from time to time, and
sentiment for independence from Mexico grew strong. The Texans

met in convention and on March 2, 1836, declared their independence, drawing on both the Declaration of Independence and the Constitution to set up a new government.

The Texans were led by Samuel Houston (1793–1863) and the Mexicans by Antonio Lopez de Santa Anna (1794–1876). Houston, who was six feet, two inches tall and liked to wear vests made of leopard skin, was born in Virginia, moved with his family to Tennessee, lived with Cherokee Indians during much of his youth and was adopted by them. Houston was elected governor of Tennessee in 1827, but when his bride suddenly left him in 1829 he resigned the governorship and went back to live with the Cherokees. Four years later he moved on to Texas, and was a delegate to the convention that declared Texas independent. A natural leader, Houston was chosen by the Texans to command their forces against Mexico. After the war for independence, Houston was elected the first president of Texas and later, after annexation, was one of its first senators.

Santa Anna, too, was a natural leader, judging by the number of times he led one faction or another in Mexico's almost continuous internal struggles. He fought first in the royalist army, then joined the fight for independence, only to turn against the leader of that struggle. He was elected president in 1833, and a year later, after another upheaval, established himself as dictator.

Even while Texas debated independence, Santa Anna and his army besieged the Alamo. The Alamo, a stone building that was originally part of a mission in San Antonio, had been converted into a fortress many years before. Now garrisoned by 187 Texans, it was besieged by 3,000 of Santa Anna's troops. From February 24 to March 6, 1836, the Texans held out, but the end came with hand-to-hand fighting inside the walls. The Mexicans killed the Texans to the last man. Among the dead were William B. Travis (1806?–1836), the commander, James Bowie (c.1796–1836) and David Crockett (1786–1836). Bowie and his brother Rezin are credited with inventing the Bowie knife, an all-purpose tool and weapon with one edge, a guarded hilt, and balanced so that it can be thrown with accuracy. Davy Crockett, already a legendary figure of frontier life, fought with Jackson against the Indians, served in Congress and pushed off to help the Texans when he became disappointed with his political career.

Less than a month later, Santa Anna's army surrounded a force of 350 Texans near Goliad, southwest of San Antonio. Vastly outnumbered, the Texans surrendered on March 20, and a week later they were shot down in cold blood. The Texans believed that Santa Anna himself ordered the massacre. These two defeats aroused the population and volunteers flocked to Sam Houston's army. Houston retreated eastward while preparing for battle and on April 21, near the San Jacinto River, attacked Santa Anna's 1,200 men with his force of about 800. The Texans, with the battle cry, "Remember the Alamo," won the battle in fifteen minutes. They killed more than 600 Mexicans and captured the rest, including Santa Anna.

The Texans made Santa Anna agree to recognize the independence of their country, but the Mexican congress repudiated the promise. Nevertheless, Texas established an independent government. At first President Jackson felt the United States should remain neutral, but on his last full day in office in March, 1837, and after Congress approved, he recognized the Texas Republic. Texas asked the United States to annex it, but when the United States did not accept the offer, Texas in the fall of 1838 withdrew the request. Forces in the United States were too evenly balanced to make a decision possible.

European nations, especially Great Britain, took an active interest in the situation. France recognized Texas as an independent nation in 1839, and Great Britain, Holland and Belgium followed the next year. Great Britain tried to mediate between Texas and Mexico to assure Texan independence. The British saw Texas as a counter-force against the United States on the American continent, and also as a source of cotton and a market for British goods. Great Britain, however, was firmly committed to the abolition of slavery, which pleased Mexico but not the Texans.

In the fall of 1843, the Tyler administration told the Texans it was ready to reopen annexation negotiations, believing the Senate would ratify such a treaty. Negotiations were completed in April, 1844, by Calhoun who was secretary of state at this time. The Senate, however, rejected the treaty in June. President Tyler tried to achieve annexation by means of a joint resolution of Congress, but the matter did not come to a vote before adjournment. When Congress met again in December, Tyler once more offered the joint resolution on annexation and this time it passed, in late February, 1845. Texas accepted the annexation terms in July, after Polk became president, and Texas was officially admitted to the Union on December 29.

When annexation became inevitable, Mexico, in March, 1845, broke off diplomatic relations with the United States. President Polk was then faced with both the possibility of war with Mexico, and an opportunity to achieve his goal of acquiring California. The specific dispute with Mexico concerned the western boundary of Texas. Mexico claimed it was the Nueces River, but Texas—although little had been done to make good the claim—insisted on the Rio Grande, about 120 miles west of the Nueces. In addition, Mexico had not made payments to Americans as agreed for damages suffered in the numerous revolutions and civil wars. In June Polk put pressure on Mexico by ordering General Zachary Taylor to advance into Texas "for the defense of the territory." At the very end of July, General Taylor established a base on the Nueces near Corpus Christi.

Polk attempted to secure California and settle other matters by peaceful means, although he was determined to have his way by war if necessary. In November, 1845, he sent John Slidell (1793–1871) as a special envoy to Mexico. Slidell, born in New York, was a prominent lawyer and politician in New Orleans and was elected to the House as a Democrat in 1843. Slidell was empowered to offer the Mexican government $5,000,000 for New Mexico and $25,000,000 for California, and to have the United States assume payment of the claims of its citizens against Mexico. Mexico would also recognize the Rio Grande as the boundary of Texas. The Mexican government refused even to receive the Slidell mission.

When word of this reached Washington on January 12, 1846, General Taylor was ordered to advance to the Rio Grande. Fighting began on April 24, when a sizable force of Mexican soldiers crossed the Rio Grande, came upon a small troop of American dragoons and surrounded them, killing several and taking the rest prisoner. Taylor sent word to Washington but the news did not reach the capital until May 9, when the cabinet was already discussing the possibility of war. Two days later Polk asked Congress to declare war, which it did, within twenty-four hours, by a large margin in each house. Congress authorized the president to call for 50,000 volunteers and appropriated $10,000,000.

General Winfield Scott was the top military commander in Washington, while General Taylor was the ranking officer facing the enemy. Polk was suspicious of both because they were Whigs and had shown an interest in politics. Either of them, as a military hero, might turn out to be the Whig's presidential candidate in 1848. Taylor (1784–1850) was born in Virginia and began a forty-year military career in 1808. He commanded ably in the War of 1812, in the Black Hawk War of 1832, and against the Seminole Indians in 1837. His looks and manners earned him the nickname "Old Rough and Ready." He did not appear impressive, being thickset, with very short legs, and a tendency to get fat. Taylor was also not neat in his dress, used rough language and looked down on military men who put too much stress on regulations and appearance. He was a true leader, possessing both a strong will and much courage.

General Taylor, with about 2,000 troops, moved westward to relieve Fort Brown, which the Mexican general, Arista, was besieging. Near Palo Alto, Texas, on May 8, Taylor attacked the enemy and they retreated. Taylor pursued and the next day caught up with the Mexican army at Resaca de la Palma. His attack routed the Mexicans who fled across the Rio Grande at Matamoros. Taylor continued to advance and on May 18, Matamoros was entered, the first Mexican city to come under American military rule.

Early in June, Taylor began another advance westward toward Monterrey, the key defensive point for the Mexicans in northern Mexico. With about 6,200 troops available, the Americans reached the outskirts of Monterrey on September 19, and on September 24, the city surrendered. The terms of the surrender allowed the Mexican army to withdraw and called for an eight-week armistice during which the Americans would not advance farther south. Polk did not like this, but Taylor's army badly needed to recuperate from the fighting and from disease which also had taken a heavy toll.

While Taylor was leading his campaign, a curious incident was taking place. Santa Anna, in one of the frequent changes of fortune in his career, had been deposed and banished in 1844. He spent his exile in Cuba, from where he led Polk to believe that if he were back in power in Mexico he would make peace with the United States. Accordingly, American naval ships were instructed to let him land in Mexico, which he did in August after the government was overthrown. Within a month Santa Anna was in command of the Mexican army, and began building it up for battle against the Americans.

Also during the summer, Colonel Stephen W. Kearny (1794–1848), who had left college to join the army in the War of 1812 and who had been an army officer ever since, was ordered to invade New Mexico from the north. He assembled a force of 1,500, mostly frontiersmen, at Fort Leavenworth, Kansas, and in June began the long march toward Santa Fe. Although Mexican forces threatened several times, they kept retreating and on August 18, surrendered Santa Fe without a battle. Kearny's men marched more than 1,000 miles in six weeks and captured an area inhabited by 80,000 people. Kearny started for California with part of his force in late September.

In seemingly subdued Santa Fe in December a carefully planned rebellion broke out. Governor Charles Bent and some other officials were assassinated and mutilated in January, 1847, before the rebellion was stamped out.

After Kearny headed for California, another part of his force left Santa Fe in October to march on El Paso and Chihuahua, a march that led 3,000 miles over mountains and through desert country. This expedition was under the command of Colonel Alexander W. Doniphan (1808–87), a Kentucky-born lawyer and soldier. Doniphan's troops first met the enemy on Christmas Day at El Brazito where they defeated a force about twice their size. El Paso surrendered and the force stayed there until February, 1847, when it set out for Chihuahua. After a march full of hardships, Doniphan's men met the Mexicans fifteen miles from Chihuahua and drove them from the field. On March 2, the Americans entered Chihuahua. An additional 600 miles of marching faced the expedition when they were ordered to join Taylor in Monterrey. From there the adventurous men of "Doniphan's Thousand" were sent home to be mustered out.

In Washington in the fall of 1846, Polk and his advisers became convinced that the way to end the war was to land American troops at Veracruz, on the Gulf of Mexico, advance inland and capture Mexico City. With some reluctance, Polk named General Scott to command this operation. Scott ordered Taylor to transfer many of his troops to the new expedition and Polk instructed Taylor to stay on the defensive. Taylor, feeling that he was being intrigued against, dispatched troops as directed to join Scott at Tampico, but disregarded his other orders and in February, 1847, began an advance toward Buena Vista, southwest of Monterrey. Santa Anna learned of the move and marched off to fight Taylor with a force of about 15,000 against the Americans' 4,800. The main fighting between the two armies took place on February 23, and was a savage battle. The next day the Mexicans retreated and the war in northern Mexico was over.

General Scott (1786–1866), who was about to take the military limelight, was a native of Virginia and had served in the army since 1808. He made a good record in the War of 1812. Scott supervised the removal of the Cherokee Indians west of the Mississippi in 1838 and for two decades, from 1841 to 1861, was commander of the United States Army. Although vain, pompous and at times undiplomatic, he was a dedicated military man who looked out for his troops' welfare. He was known to them as "Old Fuss and Feathers."

In charge of the naval forces whose task it would be to put troops ashore and help take Veracruz was Matthew Calbraith Perry (1794–1858), younger brother of Oliver Hazard Perry, a naval hero of the War of 1812. By 1837 Matthew Perry was a captain in command of one of the first steam-powered warships, where he conducted the first American school of naval-gun practice. He served for a while, starting in 1843, as commander of a squadron charged with suppressing the African slave trade.

The expedition to Veracruz got off to a slow start. Polk thought General Scott was dragging his feet, but Scott needed to build up a sufficient force and to accumulate supplies. He left Washington on November 24, 1846. In mid-March, 1847—although smallpox had broken out among his troops, which now numbered 10,000—Scott's army, with the assistance of the navy, landed unopposed on the beaches south of Veracruz. Veracruz was as strong a fortress as existed, so Scott surrounded it and besieged it with land and naval batteries. The battered city and fortress surrendered and was occupied on March 29, after a loss of only nineteen Americans.

While the siege of Veracruz was going on, Santa Anna returned from the north, suppressed opposition that was rising against him in Mexico City and organized an army to meet Scott's invasion. On April 8, the American force began its westward advance, seeking to reach the highlands where the danger of yellow fever was less. At Cerro Gordo, an easily defended mountain pass, Scott's forces met Santa Anna's on April 12, and on April 18, drove them out of their positions.

The Americans continued to advance and, on May 15, reached Puebla, seventy-five miles from the capital city. Here Scott stayed for three months to rest his troops, many of whom were ill, and to secure supplies and reinforcements. His strength was down to 7,000 men, partly because the enlistment period of some regiments was over and they started home. After rebuilding his army to 14,000 men, Scott resumed his advance. Santa Anna's opposing army numbered about 20,000. Two separate engagements on August 20, at Contreras and Churubusco, forced the Mexican army back to Mexico City's last defenses, with the Americans only three miles outside. On September 8, at the battle of Molino del Rey, the Americans drove the defenders out of a group of strongly defended buildings. It was one of the bloodiest battles; United States troops suffered over 700 casualties, including 117 killed. The most formidable strongpoint of all remained—the fortified hill of Chapultepec. The battle for it began on September 12, with an artillery bombardment, and the next day an infantry assault overwhelmed the defenders. The city itself was now assaulted, Santa Anna withdrew his beaten troops and on September 14, Mexico City surrendered.

Following the fall of Veracruz, Polk in April, 1847, tried to arrange a peace settlement with Mexico. As negotiator, he chose Nicholas P. Trist (1800–74) who was chief clerk of the State Department. Trist had studied law under Thomas Jefferson and married his granddaughter. Trist arrived in Mexico City in early May and at once got into a controversy with Scott, who felt his authority was being usurped. Within a month or so, however, the two became friendly and cooperative. During an armistice in late August and early September, Trist negotiated with the Mexicans who rejected his peace offer. By October, Polk was beginning to think he could get more out of Mexico than Trist had been instructed to demand. Trist was therefore ordered to return home, but he felt he was on the verge of reaching an agreement with a government that might collapse entirely unless the war ended.

Ignoring Washington's recall, Trist induced Santa Anna to sign a treaty on February 2, 1848, at the village of Guadalupe Hidalgo. The terms called for Mexico to recognize that Texas was part of the United States, and to cede land which included all of the later states of California, Nevada and Utah, almost all of New Mexico and Arizona, and parts of Colorado and Wyoming. In return, the United States was to pay Mexico $15,000,000 and assume the claims of its citizens against Mexico, amounting to $3,250,000.

Even though the negotiations were successful, Polk was furious with Trist for disobeying orders. He put him under arrest, took away his State Department post and refused to pay him. Not until shortly before his death did Congress vote him the money he deserved.

The president and his cabinet debated for some time whether to submit the treaty to the Senate. Polk finally decided that even though it resulted from Trist's disobedience, he had better get it ratified. By December, 1847, Congress was getting restive about the war, and with Whig strength increasing, the grumbling about the length and cost of the conflict was growing. The Senate ratified the treaty on March 10, 1848, by a margin of thirty-eight to fourteen. The war was over, at a cost of 1,721 men who were killed or died of wounds, and of another 11,155 who died of disease.

6 Oregon and California

THE OREGON country—jointly occupied by the terms of a treaty between the United States and Great Britain for a quarter of a century when President Polk took office in 1845—covered a large territory in the far northwest. It eventually became the states of Washington, Oregon and Idaho, together with parts of Montana and Wyoming, and part of the province of British Columbia in Canada. The disposition of the part of Oregon between the Columbia River on the south and the forty-ninth parallel of latitude on the north was the chief stumbling block to an agreement on a permanent division of the territory. The Democrats said flatly in 1844 that they would not compromise, and would insist that all of Oregon, up to the line of fifty-four degrees, forty minutes, become American territory. The two nations based their conflicting claims on treaties and explorations and on the activities of fur traders. Until after 1835 very few permanent settlers occupied Oregon. The farmer-pioneers who then came were mostly Americans, but they settled south of the Columbia River, primarily in the Willamette Valley.

In the John Quincy Adams administration, the United States offered to compromise by setting the boundary at the forty-ninth parallel, which would extend to the Pacific Ocean the line that ran westward to Lake of the Woods. Great Britain refused, insisting on the Columbia River line, and neither side pushed the matter until the number of American settlers increased. President Polk took the initiative, as the Democrats had promised, when he recommended to Congress in December, 1845, that the joint occupation agreement be ended, that the United States extend military protection over its citizens in Oregon and that the Oregon Trail also receive military protection. Congress approved ending the joint occupation agreement, and Polk gave England the necessary one-year's notice on May 21, 1846.

Great Britain asked the United States to renew its offer to accept the forty-ninth parallel as the boundary, but Polk, remembering his campaign pledge, did not feel he could do so. Polk was, in fact, ready to compromise because war with Mexico had been declared eight days before the treaty notification and he wanted Great Britain to remain neutral in that struggle. The Polk administration therefore indicated that if Great Britain would take the initiative, agreement could be reached. The British did so, and Polk gained Congressional approval on June 15. The forty-ninth parallel became the permanent boundary, except that Britain retained all of Vancouver Island, a portion of which lies south of the line. The United States received the larger part of the area, including the rich Columbia River Valley.

American interest in, as well as claim to, Oregon was generated by fur traders and explorers, beginning with the Lewis and Clark expedition. Reports of Oregon's wonderful features aroused the interest of missionaries and potential settlers. One of the first to catch "Oregon fever" was Hall J. Kelley (1790–1874), a New Hampshire-born teacher and railroad surveyor. In 1831 Kelley organized the American Society for Encouraging the Settlement of the Oregon Territory, petitioned Congress to assist him and issued a call for all who wanted to join to gather in St. Louis in the spring of 1832. When Congress declined to pay the expenses of such an expedition, the plan collapsed. Kelley went west by himself in 1833, traveling across Mexico and to California before reaching his goal in 1834. He got no warm greeting from the British Hudson's Bay Company officials, although they did give him shelter. Kelley became ill and, in 1835, returned to Boston, discouraged at the failure of his dream.

One of those to whom Kelley imparted his enthusiasm for Oregon was Nathaniel J. Wyeth (1802–56), a Boston businessman. Wyeth organized an 1832 expedition which was to cross the continent while a supply ship went around Cape Horn. Wyeth planned to compete with the Hudson's Bay Company in fur trading, and also to catch, preserve and send back east salmon from the Columbia River. Wyeth and his men made it across the country, but the ship was lost at sea. Wyeth tried again in 1834. He built Fort Hall on the Snake River near the present-day Pocatello, Idaho, and he took with him the Reverend Jason Lee (1803–45), a Methodist missionary who established the first mission and the first agricultural settlement in Oregon. Again, though, Wyeth was not successful. His ship arrived, but the Hudson's Bay Company competition was too strong. He returned to Boston and went into the ice business.

In 1833 a false account that four western Indians had journeyed east to St. Louis to ask for Christian missionaries for their people set off a wave of settlers toward Oregon. The first was the Reverend Lee. He was followed in 1836 by a Presbyterian missionary and physician, Marcus Whitman (1802–47), who started west in the spring with his bride, Narcissa (1808–47), and others. The party reached Oregon at the beginning of September and established a mission near the present city of Walla Walla, Washington, where on March 14, 1837, the Whitman's daughter, Alice Clarissa, became the first American white child born west of the Continental Divide. Whitman went back east in 1842 and returned the next year, bringing a large party of settlers with him. The Whitmans continued their work until November 29, 1847, when a group of Cayuse Indians, angered by the spread of white people's diseases among them, turned on the missionaries. They murdered Whitman and his wife and a dozen others.

Between the early 1840's and 1850, the flow of settlers to Oregon increased steadily and helped make good the United States' claim to the area. The first sizable group was a party of sixty-nine men, women and children who went west in 1841, about half of them ending up in Oregon and the rest in California. Two years later, 1,000 pioneers, with 1,800 cattle, set out from Independence, Missouri. They were followed by five smaller parties in 1844 and three in 1845. The next year as many as 1,350 people reached Oregon. The American population had increased by then to about 5,000, compared with only 750 British. Emigration continued and by 1850 there were 13,000 American citizens in Oregon. As early as 1843, settlers in the Willamette Valley met to set up a government to rule until the United States took over.

The route over plains and mountains that made emigration to Oregon feasible became famous as the Oregon Trail. The jumping-off place for settlers heading west was in Missouri—Independence mostly, or Westport or St. Joseph. The Trail led generally northwest up the Platte River, then along the North Platte to Fort Laramie, past Independence Rock and to South Pass in southwestern Wyoming. This pass, first used by wagons in 1832, led the emigrants through the Rocky Mountains. They then had to travel southwest to Fort Bridger. Here the Mormon Trail continued west and south, while the Oregon Trail turned back northwest, to Fort Hall on the Snake River. The California Trail at this point branched off to the southwest, and the Oregon Trail continued on to Fort Boise. After this came a hard, final climb over the Blue Mountains. It took about six months for the average emigrant train to cover the 2,000 miles of the Trail.

The Oregon Trail was not as clearly defined as a highway, and the wagon trains spread out over a fairly wide area where the land was level. At river crossings and mountain passes, the trails converged into a narrow route. Emigrants gathered at the eastern end of the trail and joined others to form wagon trains for mutual help and protection. Elijah White (1806–79), a missionary and physician who went to Oregon in 1836, helped lead the first train of more than a hundred settlers to Oregon in 1842. The trains were organized democratically, and a leader was elected. Sometimes the organization was quite elaborate, with judges, a secretary and various other functionaries. Sometimes a majority of a group became dissatisfied with the leader, voted that person out of office and elected someone else.

Good organization was necessary for the safety of all. There was danger from Indians, wild animals, storms and desert conditions. Horses and oxen had to be cared for and wagons kept in repair. At night the wagons formed a circle for protection from attack. As the miles went slowly by, many families found they had brought more furniture and household articles than the oxen could readily pull. The Oregon Trail was littered with abandoned goods, broken wagons and dead animals. Before the great trek by wagon train ended, it was also marked by the graves of about 34,000 people who never reached the promised land.

Like Oregon, California caught the imagination of Americans, and aroused desires to own the territory even before much was known about it. Until Mexico won independence from Spain in 1821, California was a distant province of the Spanish empire, under loose control from Mexico City. Spain kept all ports closed to outsiders. The Mexicans opened the ports to traders, but gave Great Britain a monopoly which expired in 1827. American merchants and ship-owners, mostly from New England, soon spotted the possibilities in trade with California. Hides and tallow were the products California offered for export, while it provided a market for manufactured goods from the United States. In a twenty-year period, one Boston firm took more than 500,000 hides out of California. As business increased, American companies established agencies and the people who ran them became the first permanent American settlers in California.

With Spain's power gone, rivalry among nations—especially the United States and Great Britain—was stimulated by the obvious usefulness of California's harbors at San Francisco, Monterey and San Diego for warships as well as merchant vessels. Efforts to acquire

California began in Jackson's administration, but offers to buy were refused. The Californians of Mexican descent were restless. Mostly people of property, they thought they would be better off as an independent nation, under the protection of England or France, or by being annexed by the United States. When Polk took office in 1845, it was clear that California would separate from Mexico, and Polk was determined to have it for the United States.

The first overland migration of American settlers to California took place in 1841, and a growing stream flowed that way thereafter. The San Joaquin Valley was colonized in 1843. By the mid-1840's, California's population consisted of about 7,500 persons of Spanish descent, about 850 Americans and a large number of docile Indians.

Among the pioneer groups that headed for California in 1846 was the ill-fated Donner party. The group was organized by two brothers, Jacob and George Donner, in Illinois. They were well-to-do and the party, numbering eighty-seven, was plentifully supplied when it set out. All went well until the group reached Fort Bridger where they followed bad advice and tried a shortcut. This trail through the Wasatch Mountains proved almost impassable, and the trek over the Salt Lake Desert exhausted them and their animals. It was September before they were in a position to cross the Sierra Nevada range. Winter snows set in and trapped them and by mid-December they were reduced to eating animal hides and tree bark. A party of eight men, five women and two Indian guides set out to try to bring back help. While they were gone, the remaining party came to the horrible realization that no one would survive unless the living practiced cannibalism on the dead. Relief did not reach them until February 19, but forty-five persons survived the long ordeal of cold and starvation.

American interest in the Far West was further stimulated in the early 1840's by the expeditions led by John C. Fremont (1813–90), explorer, soldier and politician. His career as an explorer was launched after he eloped with Jessie Benton (1824–1902), daughter of the influential senator from Missouri, Thomas Hart Benton (1782–

1858). Benton arranged for Fremont to lead an expedition into the Rocky Mountains in 1842. The next year he began a far more significant trip when he led a party into Oregon, then down the length of California and back home by a southern route. The report of this expedition, written mostly by his wife and published in 1844, increased enthusiasm for the West.

Fremont next led a foray into California, which turned out to be an important step in bringing California into the Union. With a small force he reached Monterey and set up camp in January, 1846. The Mexican officials ordered him to leave, and so Fremont marched north. He was almost at the Oregon boundary when he decided to turn back, perhaps because he received secret instructions. About this time there was dissension among the California Mexicans, reflecting turbulent conditions in Mexico. The American settlers in northern California feared one Mexican faction might win and place California under the protection of a European power. These settlers began to take countermeasures and a group seized Sonoma, northeast of San Francisco, and proclaimed the Republic of California on June 14. These Americans designed a flag with a grizzly bear and a star on it, and the event became known as the Bear Flag Revolt. Fremont, eager to be in on this revolt, arrived in Sonoma on June 25, and shortly thereafter was chosen head of the "republic."

The new nation was not independent for long. War with Mexico had begun and as soon as Commodore John D. Sloat (1781–1867)—commander of American warships in the Pacific—learned of this, he sailed for Monterey. Sending a force ashore on July 7, 1846, Sloat proclaimed California to be United States territory. Two days later another force, on Sloat's orders, seized San Francisco. Sonoma was occupied and the Bear Flag taken down in favor of the Stars and Stripes. Sloat, in ill health, was replaced by Commodore Robert F. Stockton (1795–1866) who organized a military battalion of volunteers under Fremont's command. Combined naval and land forces occupied Santa Barbara, then captured Los Angeles on August 13. Here, on

August 17, Stockton declared California annexed to the United States with himself as governor.

The issue seemed settled, but in September the Mexicans united to drive the Americans out of the important towns of southern California. While these events were taking place, Kearny, having conquered New Mexico and captured Santa Fe, had started for California with 300 men. On the way he heard that California was already won, but on arriving, he found the revolt going strong. On December 6, he defeated a Mexican force at the village of San Pascual and was able to occupy San Diego on December 12. Stockton, meantime, was preparing to advance on Los Angeles and did so on December 29. On January 8, 1847, he met and defeated a Mexican force, and entered Los Angeles two days later. The war in California was over.

American interest in California increased when, in 1848, word spread of the discovery of gold. The momentous event took place on January 24, 1848, along a branch of the American River, about forty miles from present-day Sacramento. The discoverer was James W. Marshall (1810–85) who migrated to California in 1845. He was in partnership with John A. Sutter (1803–80) to build a sawmill and was checking the project when he noticed flakes of yellow metal. Sutter was a Swiss who settled in California in 1839, became the promoter and proprietor of a colony, built Sutter's Fort and for some years ruled over his domain like a king.

The news leaked out locally, even though Sutter and Marshall tried to keep it quiet, and people swarmed into the area to look for the precious metal. On the other hand, the news traveled east slowly. First word of the discovery appeared in the New York *Herald* on August 19, 1848, but no great excitement was created until Polk included an enthusiastic account in his message to Congress on December 5.

It soon seemed that everyone, not only in the United States but in Europe, too, was determined to go look for gold. Some traveled across the continent, others took ship to the Isthmus of Panama, crossed that neck of land on muleback and boarded another ship to California. In January, 1849, 700 would-be miners tried to board a ship at Panama that had room for 250. Somehow 365 were jammed aboard. Those who were not in quite such a hurry could take a ship around Cape Horn from the east coast in somewhat more comfort. The best estimate is that in 1849 a total of 80,000 people made their way to California—55,000 of them overland and 25,000 by sea. About 5,000 who started out by the overland route never saw California, as Asiatic cholera swept through their ranks. The gold seekers who arrived found a generally chaotic situation, rough living conditions and high prices. Mining camps were raw places with only tents or shacks, a great deal of mud and some prospectors who had little respect for law and order. The camps set up their own law-enforcement machinery, usually efficient even if not too careful about legal rights. A person who committed murder was likely to be tried and shot the same day.

By the end of 1849, $10,000,000 worth of gold was mined, but a great deal of it soon left the hands of the miners. Almost all necessities had to travel the same long way the forty-niners themselves did. Miners might strike it rich, as a few did, or have a few lucky days: in eight days at one diggings five men made $1,800; two men found $17,000 worth of nuggets in one canyon; and profits of up to $500 a day for a short time were not unusual. But, the price of eggs in San Francisco went up to $10 a dozen. In a mining town a laundress could get $8 a dozen for washing shirts. San Francisco, which grew from a small village to 20,000 or more people in a few months, was a mecca for miners who wanted to spend their newfound gold on fun. The waterfront area was dubbed the Barbary Coast, after the pirate coast of North Africa, and here saloon-keepers, gamblers, prostitutes and confidence men stood ready to relieve the forty-niners of their gold dust.

One of the best accounts of the gold-rush days was written by Bayard Taylor (1825–78), a young journalist and traveler whose poetry and descriptions of his journeys made him a favorite of readers of the New York *Tribune*, which had sent him to report on the gold rush. In his *Eldorado* (1850), which consisted of his dispatches to the newspaper, he gave a vivid picture of the boom times in San Francisco. Some gamblers, he wrote, willingly paid $40,000 a year to rent a tent that was fifteen by twenty-five feet, while a young lawyer, looking for an office, was offered a cellar about twelve feet square for $250 a month. Taylor reported fifteen to thirty new houses a day being built. He also observed the nightlife and saw, among other things, a boy of fifteen win $500 gambling.

And so, before the mid-century mark was reached, the United States—with the addition of the Oregon country and California—stretched from the Atlantic to the Pacific, and 1,000 miles or more from north to south. It was the heyday of manifest destiny.

7 The West: Old and New

THE UNITED STATES in 1825 included two "wests." One was the Old Northwest—that region west of the Allegheny Mountains, north of the Ohio River and east of the Mississippi, which became part of the nation when the war for independence was won. The other west was the even larger and mostly unsettled territory west of the Mississippi acquired by the Louisiana Purchase of 1803.

American pioneers pushed into the Old Northwest soon after the Revolution, and population increased steadily. The opening of the Erie Canal across New York State in 1825 gave a new impetus to migration because farm products of the fertile land could be shipped profitably to eastern markets. By 1830, for example, Ohio had four times as many people as in 1810. The population of Indiana doubled between 1830 and 1840, while the next territory west, Illinois, tripled from 157,000 to 476,000. Detroit was a boomtown in 1831, and when Michigan was admitted to statehood in 1837, it was settled as far north as Saginaw and Grand Rapids. More than a third of all Americans, 6,376,000, lived west of the Alleghenies by 1840. Many of the settlers were immigrants: when Wisconsin became a state in 1848, nearly a third of its 305,000 people were foreign born—mostly Germans and Scandinavians.

The great surge westward carried with it land speculators, promoters of new towns and the accompanying salespeople, lawyers and bankers. Tracts of land were acquired and towns laid out with streets and plots for stores and homes. These "town lots" were sold to people back east who believed they would become wealthy real-estate owners, but who soon found out that the "town" consisted of nothing but a map.

Among the pioneers who made practical contributions to the settlement of the Old Northwest were Henry L. Ellsworth (1791–1858) and Morris Birkbeck (1764–1825). Ellsworth, a lawyer and business-man, went west in 1832 as one of the commissioners supervising the removal of Indians to Oklahoma. He was accompanied by the author Washington Irving. His interest in the west aroused, Ellsworth purchased 18,000 acres of land in Indiana and issued a booklet promoting settlement in the Wabash Valley. He was appointed commissioner of patents in 1835 and held the post for ten years, after which he went on with his Indiana venture until he owned 100,000 acres. In 1837, while commissioner, he began the free distribution of seeds, and in 1839 persuaded Congress to make a first appropriation of $1,000 to gather agricultural statistics. Birkbeck was an Englishman who had worked to improve agriculture there before he came to the United States in 1817. He brought with him £18,000 to invest in farmland and some prize livestock. Birkbeck acquired thousands of acres in Illinois and founded the town of Albion in 1818.

Explorers and fur traders were gradually mapping the new west across the Mississippi, but in 1825 much of it was yet uncharted. Along the river, permanent settlement was already fairly extensive. Missouri became a state as early as 1821, and Iowa was opened to settlement in 1833. The planter economy of the South thinly settled the western side of the river, particularly in Arkansas. Beyond the fertile land near the Mississippi, however, lay an almost unimaginable expanse of plains, nearly bare of trees and in places little better than desert. Francis Parkman, American historian, saw the plains and wrote in *The Oregon Trail*:

> One day we rode on for hours, without seeing a tree or a bush: before,
> behind, and on either side, stretched the vast expanse, rolling in a

succession of graceful swells, covered with the unbroken carpet of fresh green grass. Here and there a crow, a raven, or a turkey-buzzard, relieved the uniformity.

West of the ninety-eighth meridian of longitude—which runs through eastern South Dakota in the north and just east of central Texas in the south—the Great Plains received only ten to twenty inches of rainfall a year, insufficient to sustain the kind of agriculture practiced on eastern farmlands. Beyond the Great Plains were the Rocky Mountains, far higher and more difficult to penetrate than the Alleghenies, while between the Rockies and the Sierra Nevada lay the Great Basin, a rugged, very dry region. The area immediately east of the Rockies, taking in a good deal of the Great Plains, became known as the Great American Desert, and although it is not actually a desert it retained that reputation for most of the nineteenth century. It was, indeed, a frightening region to cross—transportation being as slow as it was and travelers having to carry their food with them or starve. In his book *Astoria* (1836), Washington Irving wrote:

> It is a land where no man permanently abides; for, in certain seasons of the year there is no food either for the hunter or his steed. The herbage is parched and withered; the brooks and streams are dried up; the buffalo, the elk and the deer have wandered to distant parts, keeping within the verge of expiring verdure, and leaving behind them a vast uninhabited solitude, seamed by ravines, the beds of former torrents, but now serving only to tantalize and increase the thirst of the traveler.

One of the features of the Great Plains, both as a unique sight and as a valuable economic resource, was the bison, a hoofed, short-horned animal with large humped shoulders. The bison, often called the buffalo, roamed the plains in enormous herds and were valuable to Indians and white men for their hides and for food. They were hunted from horseback and in the 1840's hundreds of thousands of them were killed every year. There may have been as many as 15,000,000 of them at that time, but they were slaughtered faster than they could reproduce.

The traders and settlers who moved west usually traveled over fairly well-defined routes, such as the Oregon Trail. The California Trail branched off from the Oregon Trail at Fort Hall and led southwest. It followed the Humboldt River most of the way to the Sierra Nevada. After crossing those mountains, usually through Truckee Pass, the pioneer could turn north up the Sacramento Valley or south into the San Joaquin Valley. The wagon the emigrants used on their long journey to Oregon or California was not as large as the famous Conestoga wagon of the east. It was ten feet long and eight and a half feet high from the road to the top of its canvas roof. Such a wagon could carry a ton of goods and was normally drawn by six oxen.

The Santa Fe Trail was a heavily used trade route, running from Independence, Missouri, to Santa Fe, New Mexico. It became a profitable route for American merchants after 1821 when Mexico won its independence. The Spanish rulers had discouraged foreigners from entering their territory. The trail led up the Arkansas River and then crossed the Cimarron Desert, a fifty-mile wide expanse of barren sand that drove both men and beasts mad with thirst if they ran out of water. After this the trail followed the Cimarron River to Bent's Fort where it turned south, went through Raton Pass and on to Santa Fe. The early traders suffered attacks by Indians, and so they began to all travel together in one annual caravan. The 1824 caravan set out in May with twenty-five wagons which carried goods worth $30,000, and was guarded by eighty-one men. Six years later the caravan consisted of sixty wagons and twice as many men. The next year the caravan was still bigger and carried goods worth $200,000. In spite of precautions, the 1829 caravan was attacked by fifty Comanche Indians on horseback. They were beaten off with the loss of one man.

The fur trade, consisting chiefly of beaver-trapping, was an important, although declining, element in the exploration and the economy of the West. Its center was along the upper reaches of the Missouri River and its tributaries. Here, and farther west in Oregon,

Americans and British were strong competitors. John Jacob Astor and his American Fur Company, which by 1822 dominated the eastern fur trade around the Great Lakes, moved across the Mississippi in 1827 with the purchase of the Columbia Fur Company. Astor gave Kenneth McKenzie (1801–61)—a native of Scotland who had been president of the Columbia outfit and was one of the ablest traders—the task of securing a monopoly, by any means, of the trade on the upper Missouri.

McKenzie first built Fort Union at the mouth of the Yellowstone River, where it runs into the Missouri in North Dakota. He was then in a position to operate in untouched beaver country—if he could pacify the Blackfoot Indians, who had a reputation for hating the white man. Risking his life, he and others went into Blackfoot country and secured an agreement. As a result, a trading party that went among the Indians in 1831 returned the next spring with more than 4,000 beaver pelts.

The Rocky Mountain Fur Company competed with Astor's firm, while the Hudson's Bay Company, moving some of its operations eastward, also tried to get a share of the Missouri fur trade. The result was too much trapping and a steady decline in the number of pelts. In 1833 and 1834 catches were small, and the American Fur Company bought out the Rocky Mountain Fur Company. Fewer trappers brought fewer pelts to the annual summer rendezvous. There the skins were traded for supplies for the next season, and there the trappers usually drank up and gambled away a good deal of the money they received for their winter's work. The last rendezvous was held in 1840.

People who were active in exploring the West in the quarter-century from 1825 to 1850 included Kit Carson (1809–68), James Ohio Pattie (1804–50?) and Benjamin L. E. de Bonneville (1796–1878). Carson ran away from his job as a saddler's apprentice to join a caravan to Santa Fe in 1826. He went on to Taos, which he made his headquarters, and acted as guide and hunter for exploring parties. He accompanied Fremont on expeditions and it was Fremont's glowing reports of Carson's skill and courage that made him famous. While guiding Kearny's force to California, Carson and two others got through enemy lines at night to bring Kearny's small force some badly needed help. Carson became a folk hero while still alive, and much was written about him. Of one biography, he said that the author "laid it on a leetle too thick."

Pattie, a Kentucky-born explorer and trapper, made several difficult trips in the southwest between 1824 and 1830. His *Personal Narrative* (1831) helped spread word of the West. Pattie's greatest exploit was the trip he took in the late 1820's when there was a smallpox epidemic in California. The Mexican authorities asked him to visit almost every settlement from San Diego to San Francisco because he had a small supply of vaccine. He is said to have vaccinated 23,000 persons, making live vaccine as needed from those already inoculated. He was promised one dollar a patient, but there was a squabble over the terms of the agreement and Pattie never collected.

Bonneville, born in France, was a graduate of West Point. He took two years' leave from the army in 1832 and, with financial backing secured in New York, set out with 110 men to become a fur trader in the Green River country of Wyoming and Utah. Bonneville was a failure as a trader, but he was another of the colorful figures who opened up the West. He took the first wagon train through South Pass, and he produced maps that gave the first reliable information about some parts of the West.

The unknown West also lured people from Europe. Prince Maxmilian of Wied-Neuwied, who fought against Napoleon in the Prussian army and later spent two years in naturalist studies in Brazil, came to the United States in 1833. He traveled far up the Missouri on boats of the American Fur Company and wrote a book about his experiences. Joseph N. Nicollet (1786–1843) was a French mathematician and somewhat of a prodigy. He was unfortunate in some financial ventures and came to America in 1832. Soon the West fascinated him, too, and in 1836–37 he led an expedition seeking the source of the Mississippi River. The Federal government sponsored an expedition up the Missouri in 1838–39, on which Nicollet was accompanied by the young Fremont. He was the first to make careful observations of altitude in the West.

Pierre Jean De Smet (1801–73) was born in Belgium, came to the United States where he was ordained in 1827, and spent a long career as a Jesuit missionary to the Indians. He began his work at Council Bluffs, Iowa in 1838. Two years later he went to Montana to work among the Flathead Indians after two of them traveled all the way to St. Louis seeking a "black robe." He established missions in Montana and Idaho, won the friendship of a number of tribes and at times mediated between whites and Indians.

More anonymously than explorers such as Fremont, the men of the Army's Corps of Topographical Engineers contributed to the opening of the West. They drew the first scientific map of the Great Salt Lake in 1850, were the first to explore the floor of the Grand Canyon on foot, and began the study of archeology in the southwest by calling attention to the remains of Indian civilization there.

A man who never went west had as much to do with the winning of the West as any explorer or soldier. He was Samuel Colt (1814–72), an inventor born in Connecticut. In the West the only way of getting anywhere very fast—whether for peaceful purposes or to fight Indians or hunt—was by horseback. The weapons of the East, especially the long rifle, were unsatisfactory when the user was mounted on a horse. The rifle was too bulky and reloading took too long. Pistols were handier but they, too, carried only one shot at a time. When Colt in 1835–36 devised and patented a revolving breach pistol that held six shots, the perfect weapon for the West came into being. Colt started a factory to produce the pistols, but the firm failed in 1842. The weapon, however, earned a reputation in Texas and its popularity grew. When the Mexican War started, Colt received an order for 1,000 pistols from the government and from then on his factory produced thousands.

The American West, new or old, struck everyone as entirely different from the long-established East. Harriet Martineau, after her visit from England, wrote of the Old Northwest:

> The traveller should go into the west when he desires to see universal freedom of manners. The people of the west have a comfortable self-complacency, equally different from the arrogance of the south, and the timidity of the north. They seem to unite with this the hospitality which distinguishes the whole country: so that they are, on the whole, a very bewitching people.

An American from the East, Mary A. Holley, while visiting Texas in 1831, encouraged newcomers:

> He will find, here, abundant exercise for all his faculties, both of body and mind, a new stimulus to his exertions, and a new current for his affections. He may be obliged to labour hard, but riches are a very certain reward of his exertions. . . . If he have a just ambition, he will glow with generous pride, while he is marking out an untrodden path, acting in an unhackneyed sphere, and founding for himself, and his children after him, a permanent and noble independence.

8   The Indians' Long Trail

THE ACTIVITIES of trappers, explorers and traders on the Great Plains and in the Rocky Mountains brought the Indians of the Far West into close contact with white Americans for the first time. East of the Mississippi, the Indians had been declining in numbers and surrendering land to the whites for many years. President Jackson summed up the problem in his first message to Congress in December, 1829. He pointed out that the two main aspects of the current policy were contradictory: on the one hand, attempts were made to "civilize" the Indians and turn them into settled farmers; on the other, they were being uprooted from their land and forced to migrate west.

Jackson favored removal. He proposed that a large territory be set aside west of the Mississippi River where all tribes would be allocated their own land. The tribes would be self-governing, their land would be guaranteed forever, and the Federal government would step in only if necessary to preserve peace. In furtherance of the removal policy, the Jackson administration in eight years concluded ninety-four treaties with Indian tribes whereby they gave up their traditional land and agreed to migrate west. The Indian Removal Act of 1830 appropriated $500,000 to move Indians. They were to be compensated for any improvements on their present land and for moving costs, and were to receive land across the Mississippi. The Indian Trade and Intercourse Act of 1834 redefined the territory where the Indians were to have "perpetual" protection and provided that a ring of forts be built around the area to keep the Indians in and the whites out.

The first tribe to be moved west under the 1830 law was the Choctaw of Mississippi. They signed a treaty in 1830 and about 4,000 of them began the march in November, 1831. The weather turned very cold and the money the government was to provide for expenses of the trip arrived late. After much suffering, the Choctaws reached the new Indian territory in 1832 and were settled in what became southeastern Oklahoma, near the Texas and Arkansas borders. It was marshy land and the Choctaws did not fare well. They were the first of the Five Civilized Tribes to be moved to Oklahoma, the others being the Chickasaw, Cherokee, Creek and Seminole Indians.

Next to go were the Creeks. The Creeks were a settled, agricultural people, with about fifty towns in their territory. An 1832 treaty ceded their land to the government, but chiefs and heads of families could keep homestead allotments if they so desired. Removal was not called for, but the continued pressure of whites, and the fraudulent methods they used to take over the allotments, made life impossible for the Creeks. The trouble between the Creeks and unscrupulous whites grew so bad that the government took the easy way out by ordering the removal of the Creeks in 1836. They were harassed and cheated on the long march, and an unsafe steamboat sank drowning 311 of the 2,000 who started. Only half the tribe survived the migration and the early years in Oklahoma. The Chickasaws of northern Mississippi signed removal treaties in 1832 and 1834, but did not go west until 1837. They arranged for the government to sell the land they gave up and to hold the money for a council of the tribe, so they fared better than other Indians. The Chickasaws owned thousands of horses which they took with them, although white horse thieves stole some on the way.

The Cherokee Indians, dwelling mostly in Georgia, were the largest and most important of the tribes of the southeast. In 1827 they established the Cherokee Nation, with its own constitution. The

Cherokees were prosperous agriculturalists and many owned slaves. They had their own written language and their own schools. The Georgians were eager to drive the Cherokees off their land and after gold was discovered in 1828, trouble began in earnest. Georgia attempted to put the Cherokees under state law, but the Indians contended only the Federal government had authority over them. A Supreme Court decision in 1832, under Chief Justice Marshall, upheld this contention and overruled the Georgia law. When it was announced, President Jackson is supposed to have said: "John Marshall has made his decision. Now let him enforce it."

A small Cherokee faction signed a removal treaty in 1835, but most of the tribe held stubbornly to their lands until 1838 when the Van Buren administration decided the only solution to the struggle between the Georgia whites and the Indians was to move the latter across the Mississippi by force. General Scott was sent with troops to carry out the decision. Under armed guard, about 15,000 Cherokees started west. Troubled by sickness, poor food and bad weather, about 4,000 died on the way.

The last of the Civilized Tribes, the Seminoles of Florida, fought a seven-year war with the United States before being removed to Oklahoma. A treaty was signed in 1832 providing for removal within three years, but many of the Seminoles repudiated the treaty. Their leader was Osceola (c.1800–38), whose father was white. When he and some of his followers killed an agent sent by Washington to supervise the removal of the Seminoles, Federal troops were dispatched to Florida and a war began that lasted until August, 1842. The war cost the United States 1,500 soldiers killed, and at least $20,000,000. In 1837, American troops seized Osceola while he was negotiating under a flag of truce. He was shut up in a prison at Fort Moultrie, South Carolina, where he died in a few months. After they gave up the fight, most of the Seminoles moved to Oklahoma, but a sizable band refused and hid out in the Everglades. In all, about 60,000 of the five tribes were moved by 1850.

Another war, of shorter duration, marked the attempt to remove the Sac and Fox Indians from the Old Northwest in 1832. The Sac and Fox were led by Chief Black Hawk (1767–1838), who fought on the side of the British in the War of 1812. When squatters moved in on his land, even plowing up the graves of the tribe's ancestors, Black Hawk reluctantly led his tribesmen across the Mississippi into Missouri. There they were threatened by both famine and hostile Sioux Indians. Badly in need of food, the Sac and Fox recrossed the Mississippi in the spring of 1832, hoping to find some land on which they could plant corn. The whites assumed this was a hostile expedition and the Illinois militia was called out. Federal troops were also sent. The Indians were cornered and most were massacred, including women and children. Black Hawk was captured and after being kept in prison for a time, he was taken on a tour of eastern cities, and was eventually presented to President Jackson in the White House.

The Winnebago Indians of Wisconsin were moved several times. They fought against the Americans in both the Revolution and the War of 1812, and secretly helped Black Hawk in 1832. The Winnebagos agreed in 1837 to move west, and by the 1840's some were settled in Nebraska but many remained in Wisconsin. They numbered about 4,500, far fewer than in 1800.

While the Indians of the East were losing their homes, those of the trans-Mississippi region were experiencing the inevitable encroachment of white civilization on their way of life. The culture of these Indians was predominantly that of the Plains Indians. Several centuries before, they were fewer in number and lived in the more fertile regions where some agriculture could be practiced. Beginning in the sixteenth century, however, these Indians acquired horses and gained skill in using them. The first horses in the region were those that escaped from the Spanish explorers. Gradually the number of horses increased, and so did the Indians' reliance on them. By the late eighteenth century a new culture, organized around the horse, was typical of the Plains Indians. With the horse they were able to abandon their primitive agriculture and rely on hunting. The buffalo was the prime prey of the Indian hunters and, as Francis Parkman noted in *The Oregon Trail*, it

> supplies them with the necessaries of life; with habitation, food, clothing, beds, and fuel; strings for their bows, glue, thread, cordage; trail-ropes for their horses, coverings for their saddles, vessels to hold water, boats to cross streams, and the means of purchasing all that they want from traders. When the buffalo are extinct, they too must dwindle away.

The Plains Indians became what most Americans thought all Indians had always looked like: a young brave in war paint, his bonnet trailing a tail of feathers, mounted on horseback with bow and arrow or rifle, furiously attacking a wagon train of pioneers. The Plains culture was a male-dominated society—as Parkman indicates in two more of his colorful descriptions, that of what he calls "a man of distinction," and the sights and sounds of an Indian tent village being erected on a new site:

> His head was shaved and painted red, and from the tuft of hair remaining on the crown dangled several eagle's feathers, and the tails of two or three rattlesnakes. His cheeks, too, were daubed with vermilion; his ears were adorned with green glass pendants; a collar of grizzly bears' claws surrounded his neck, and several large necklaces of wampum hung on his breast . . . .
>
> Some of the lodges were already set up, or the squaws perhaps were busy in drawing the heavy coverings of skin over the bare poles. Others were as yet mere skeletons, while others still, poles, covering and all, lay scattered in disorder on the ground among buffalo robes, bales of meat, domestic utensils, harness, and weapons. Squaws were screaming to one another, horses rearing and plunging, dogs yelping, eager to be disburdened of their loads, while the fluttering of feathers and the gleam of savage ornaments added liveliness to the scene.
>
> The small children ran about amid the crowd, while many of the boys were scrambling among the overhanging rocks, and standing with their little bows in their hands, looking down upon the restless throng. In

contrast with the general confusion, a circle of old men and warriors sat in the midst, smoking in profound indifference and tranquility.

The Indians were disturbed by the growing number of wagon trains that crossed their territory because the pioneers destroyed such timber as there was, and drove off the buffalo. This goaded the Indians into attacking the trains. In turn, the Federal government took steps to protect emigrants by establishing forts garrisoned with army forces.

Different tribes reacted in different ways to the white invasion, and they suffered different fates. The Sioux Indians—who were at the height of their power in the middle of the eighteenth century when they numbered at least 30,000—inhabited the northern Great Plains and western prairies in Wisconsin, Iowa, Minnesota and North and South Dakota. They signed treaties with the United States in 1815 and 1825, and caused little trouble during the period to 1850. The Mandan Indians were visited as early as 1804 by the Lewis and Clark expedition and were friendly. They were almost wiped out in 1837 when a smallpox epidemic swept through the tribe. In six months it killed all but about 100 out of 1,600.

The Pawnee Indians in Nebraska were fierce fighters against other tribes, although they never fought United States forces. Located along the Oregon Trail, they stole cattle and horses from the passing pioneers. They sometimes threatened to attack the emigrants unless given gifts, and on occasion killed a few whites. The Pawnees were outstanding among tribes for their ritual and myth. They practiced human sacrifice, killing a captive maiden to propitiate Morning Star, the rising and dying god of vegetation. Smallpox and cholera in the 1830's and 1840's greatly reduced their numbers.

In the southwest dwelt the Kiowa, Apache, Comanche, Navaho and Mohave tribes. Forced south over the years, the Kiowas lived in northern Texas and Oklahoma, near the Apaches and the Comanches. Allied with the Comanches, they raided Mexicans, Texans and other Indian tribes. They were forced in 1837 to sign a treaty in which they promised to let white people travel through their lands. The Apaches were fierce and cruel warriors who attacked whites along the western part of the Santa Fe Trail. As more whites entered their territory, relations with the Apaches worsened. The Comanches of Texas, who were perhaps the most warlike of all tribes, raided traffic on the Santa Fe Trail as early as the 1820's. They probably killed more whites in relation to their numbers than any other tribe. They seem also to have introduced the peyote ritual to the Plains tribes.

The Navahos in Arizona were enemies of the Pueblo Indians, whom they raided many times. Later they attacked Spanish and Mexican settlements in New Mexico and, when the Americans took over the territory in 1846, they fought them, too, killing the first government agent. The Navahos lived in earth-covered lodges in the winter and brush dwellings in the summer. After the Spaniards introduced sheep, they became noted sheep raisers. The Mohave tribe lived along the Colorado River in Arizona and California, and its members were semi-sedentary farmers who built low brush dwellings. They almost wiped out a party led by Jedediah Smith (1799–1831), one of the most famous of the mountainmen, when the group came through in 1827 on the way to California. The Mohaves were seeking revenge for indignities an earlier group of trappers had inflicted on them.

In the far northwest lived the Nez Percé, Flathead, Blackfoot and Cayuse tribes. The Nez Percés, in western Idaho and northern Oregon, were so named by the French, although not many of them seem to have worn nose pendants. There were about 6,000 of them in the 1830's, and at that time they asked for Christian missionaries. They lived chiefly by catching salmon and digging roots, but they later adopted many of the Plains Indians traits and became excellent horse breeders. The Flathead Indians who lived in the Bitterroot River Valley of western Montana did not have flat heads. Adjacent tribes flattened the fronts of their heads to create a pointed appearance at the top and so, by contrast, this tribe seemed flatheaded. Lewis and Clark thought there were about 600 of them early in the century, but war with the Blackfeet over hunting land reduced their numbers to about 350. The Blackfeet, who lived along the upper Missouri River, were usually hostile to whites. The only crop they cultivated was tobacco which they grew for ceremonial purposes. After the Cayuse Indians of Oregon and Washington murdered Marcus Whitman at his mission, a group of settlers made war on the Cayuse and subdued them. The Cayuse bred a small horse that became so well known all Indian ponies were called cayuses.

The Indians of California suffered a different introduction to white civilization than that of the Plains Indians. The two cultures met in 1769 when the Spaniards began colonizing California and the first Franciscan mission was established. About 200,000 Indians lived in the area then. Divided into many tribes, they were an unwarlike, hunting and fishing people. The Franciscans brought about 25,000 of them into the missions where they were taught crafts and farming, but they lost their own religion and customs. The Spanish army kept them virtual prisoners to grow food for the soldiers and the mortality rate was exceedingly high. When the Mexican government in 1833 secularized the missions, the Indians were supposed to benefit by receiving land. In fact, though, the missions became the property of large landholders and the Indians were either scattered and left to their own inadequate resources, or reduced to little better than slaves on the ranches. When the United States took over California and when the gold rush brought thousands of people to the region, the Indians were treated even worse and were murdered at will. By 1850 the Indian population was reduced to between 110,000 and 130,000.

Nearly 100,000 eastern Indians were moved west of the Mississippi by 1850. The land given them was often inadequate for raising crops and many of the Indians refused to adapt to an agricultural life. Indians of mixed blood clashed with the full bloods; the older emigrants resented the newer ones. The western tribes did not like the removal policy because it created competition for the buffalo. The eastern and western tribes fought each other, the former holding their own against the supposedly fiercer Plains Indians. As for the Plains Indians, while they freely roamed the region in 1850, their way of life was already waning. Disease took a heavy toll and the fur trade was nearly ended, leaving the Indians dependent on the white man's goods to which they had become accustomed.

9 Industry and Commerce

EXCEPT FOR the depression that followed the Panic of 1837, the quarter century from 1825 to 1850 was one of steady growth in manufacturing and commerce. New plants and new industries sprang up, largely in the northeast, while American merchant ships profitably sailed the oceans.

As time went on, more goods were produced in large factory buildings, using machinery run by water or steam power. During much of the period, manufacturers were dependent on water power to run their machines and on water transportation to move their goods to market. Steam power gradually replaced water power, although it was more expensive. Six large textile mills in Massachusetts used steam power in 1850. As long as water power was used, factories were built in rural surroundings rather than in cities, and while this disturbed the landscape it made working conditions more pleasant.

The flow of domestic commerce increased, and covered a larger area. The West shipped foodstuffs to the North and the South, and bought manufactured goods from the North. The South shipped its staple raw materials, particularly cotton, to the North and to Great Britain via the northern ports. In return, the South bought factory products from the North. The eastern ports imported foreign goods which merchants distributed all over the land. When firewood became scarce, bulky shipments of soft coal from Virginia and hard coal from Pennsylvania were sent to heat homes in the cities and to run factory machinery. The timber-growing areas shipped quantities of lumber to the cities where buildings went up every day. The growing flow of goods was sustained by steamboats, canals and the new railroad system. Traffic on the Erie Canal, which was high in 1836, doubled by 1847, while the Mississippi River trade nearly doubled in the same period.

A new kind of American businessman developed who was as much community booster as private entrepreneur, and who was usually active in real estate and transportation. Such a person was William B. Ogden (1805–77). Born in a small town in New York State, he was already dealing in real estate when he was fifteen. He agitated to get the state to aid the construction of the New York and Erie Railroad, but in 1835, when the money was appropriated, he moved on to Chicago where he saw a broader field for his talents. Two years later, when Chicago was incorporated, Ogden was elected its first mayor. He made a great deal of money in Chicago real estate (one property he bought in 1845 for $15,000 was worth $10,000,000 twenty years later) and he also worked to improve the city with a sewage system, parks and a medical college, among other facilities and institutions.

The textile industry was the first to develop on a sizable scale, and in this period it remained the largest. More than two-thirds of all cotton manufacturing was in New England, where by 1850 there were 564 plants, capitalized at more than $58,000,000 and employing 61,893 operators. The South, by contrast, had 166 plants, capitalized at $7,250,000 and using 10,043 workers. The New England textile industry at first employed female workers, most of them young farm girls.

Young girls were first employed at Waltham, Massachusetts, but the so-called Waltham System reached its peak in the mills of Lowell in the same state. The company erected rooming houses where the girls lived, and although they were somewhat crowded, conditions were no worse than in many city homes and on farms. The company also provided churches, a library and other features of a town. The girls received from $2.50 to $3.00 a week, from which about $1.25 was deducted for room and board. They worked long hours, and their time and conduct outside of work were strictly regulated. They stayed at the mills four and a half years on the average and then went home, usually having saved some money for a dowry so they could get married. In the 1840's conditions grew worse when the mill owners of New England banded together to reduce wages, keep up long hours and use blacklists to weed out anyone who misbehaved. There were 6,300 female workers in the Lowell textile factories in 1845 and 2,915 males. By the middle 1840's male operatives, mostly French-Canadian and Irish immigrants, were fast replacing the girls.

A number of enterprising people tried to increase cotton manu- facturing in the South, but the slave economy and a general suspicion of factories hindered their efforts. A few mills were built, and one established in 1825 used slave labor. William Gregg (1800–67) argued that more southern industry would keep the North from dominating the region. He established a model factory at Graniteville, South Carolina, in 1846 and around it built the first southern mill town. He used local labor, bringing in poor white families, and by 1850 employed 325 of them. He established a social welfare system that was in advance of its time, but he had little success in enlarging southern industry as a whole.

Factory production of woolen goods lagged behind cotton, and the industry was not much more than half the size. American manufacturers found it difficult to compete with the British product, and since most farms raised sheep, woolen cloth continued to be produced at home. Finally, the existing textile machinery did not work as well with wool as with cotton. As late as 1830 in New England more woolen cloth was woven at home than in factories. The situation changed after 1840 when a power loom was devised that could weave figures and patterns.

Iron was smelted in small quantities and in scattered locations in colonial times, but it was not until the second quarter of the nineteenth century that iron was produced on a large scale. New processes made it possible to use coal instead of charcoal in smelting operations. The output was 165,000 tons of iron in 1830, 300,000 tons in 1840 and 650,000 tons by 1846–47. More iron products were produced by machinery instead of by hand: railroad spikes in 1825; shovels, spades and axes in 1826; horseshoes in 1835. The use of anthracite coal for heating boosted the demand for iron stoves and by 1850 over 300,000 were produced annually. By that time, too, about half the iron industry was located in Pennsylvania, near the coal supply.

Among the pioneers in business and industry who were behind the nation's economic growth, and who made fortunes in the process, were John Jacob Astor (1763–1848), Peter Cooper (1791–1883) and Cornelius Vanderbilt (1794–1877). Astor, who was born in Germany, was penniless when he arrived in the United States in 1784. Starting with a small shop that sold musical instruments and furs, Astor rapidly branched out. By the turn of the century, his chartered ships were profitably sailing the oceans, especially in the China trade. When he went into the fur trade, he built up his American Fur Company until it was practically a monopoly. Meanwhile, his investments in New York City real estate were fabulously profitable and he made more money helping finance the War of 1812.

Peter Cooper also had wide-ranging business interests, but took more interest in philanthropy and public service than did Astor. Cooper first made money in the glue business, then turned to iron manufacturing. He designed and built *Tom Thumb*, one of the first locomotives constructed in the United States. With his son and son-in-law, he opened a rolling mill in Trenton in 1845, and rolled the first structural iron for fireproof buildings. Cornelius Vanderbilt made his first fortune in shipping, and after the Civil War went into the railroad field and made more millions. At the age of sixteen he bought a small boat and ran a passenger and freight service between New

York City and Staten Island. Vanderbilt expanded his shipping interests around New York and up the Hudson River to such an extent that he became known as Commodore Vanderbilt. During the gold rush he obtained a concession for a water and road route across Nicaraugua that enabled him to take business away from shipowners who were using the longer route by way of Panama.

In the Jacksonian period, manufacturing increased—not only in quantity and value, but also in the scale of operation. Factories grew bigger and used more employees. This in turn separated the owner and employer from the workers. Larger units of production and power machinery made it possible to perform all steps in a process under one roof, from raw materials to finished goods. Mass production and the assembly-line system began here. Larger amounts of capital than before were needed, and investments in American factories grew from $50,000,000 to $250,000,000 between 1820 and 1840. Most of the new capital was supplied by people who previously made their money by investing in shipping and mercantile ventures in general. An indirect effect was an increase in the use of the corporate form of business organization. At the start of the period, each corporate charter had to be secured by a separate act of a state legislature. The Jacksonians wanted to make the corporation form available to all entrepreneurs, so general laws under which anyone could set up a corporation by meeting certain requirements were enacted. The first modern corporation law was that of Connecticut in 1837.

Visiting the United States in the middle of the period, Tocqueville thought that the American "manufacturing aristocracy" was among the harshest he knew of, but he felt that it was at that time sufficiently confined by the government. He believed, though, that if permanent inequality ever came to America it would be through manufacturing, and he urged the friends of democracy to keep a sharp eye on the march of industrialism.

Ocean shipping and the import-export business, important since colonial times, continued to prosper. The American merchant fleet was large, the country had many raw materials to export and needed—although in decreasing quantities—manufactured products from abroad. Except for the 1840's, imports exceeded exports in each decade. The deficit in the balance of payments with other countries was made up largely by the profits earned by the merchant marine, and by heavy investment of foreign capital in the United States.

Even though textile manufacturing was expanding, cotton and woolen goods were still the most important imports between 1825 and 1850. Among exports, raw cotton was the most important product America shipped abroad, accounting for more than half the value of all exports. The total value of American foreign trade in 1825 was $181,000,000; twenty-five years later it had increased to $318,000,000. Great Britain was both the best customer and the largest supplier.

This period marked the heyday of the wooden sailing ship, and both their size and numbers increased remarkably. In the early 1840's, a cargo ship of 1,000 tons was large, but within a decade it had become typical. American ships had several advantages: building costs were lower, American sailors were believed to be the most competent, and they were able to operate ships with smaller crews. Packet ships were popular and speeded up ocean travel. These sailing ships were built for speed and they left port on regular schedules, down to the day and hour. A packet made the run from New York to Liverpool in about twenty days, but against the prevailing winds it took about thirty-five days for the return trip. For $150 a passenger could have a cabin and good food; for $30 he could have a bunk in steerage if he brought his own food and bedding.

Foremost among sailing ships of the world for speed and beauty were the American clipper ships, first developed in the 1830's and holding their own for some time after steamships plied the oceans. The clipper was a very long and narrow ship with an enormous area of sail. Most such ships were built at Baltimore and in New England. The first true clipper was the *Ann McKim*, completed in 1833. Donald McKay (1810–80), born in Nova Scotia, established a shipyard in

Boston in 1845 and was the leading builder, both of very large sailing ships and of clipper ships. One of his ships, the *Flying Cloud*, covered 374 miles in one day. The clippers set speed records all over the world, but their success led the United States to be slow in applying steam power to ocean vessels and in building ships with iron hulls. The British took the lead in these respects as the 1840's ended.

American merchants and shipowners had been busy in the Pacific Ocean since the late eighteenth century. The profitable and exotic China trade brought furniture, jewelry and art to America. In 1832 the government sent Edmund Roberts, a merchant, to the Far East to negotiate with several rulers. Roberts returned in 1836 with trade treaties with the Sultan of Muscat and the King of Siam, the first between the United States and far eastern nations. For many years China allowed foreigners to trade only at the port of Canton, but after the British won the Opium War of 1842, China was forced to open up five more ports. The United States dispatched Caleb Cushing (1800–79) to seek equal opportunity for American traders. Cushing was a lawyer and a member of the House for eight years. In 1844 he negotiated the Treaty of Wanghia, by which the Chinese emperor promised to treat the United States as well as any other nation.

American fishing vessels operated in both the Atlantic and the Pacific, cod fishing being important in the North Atlantic. The most venturesome sea quest, though, was the search for whales and their valuable oil. The greatest whaling period began in 1820 and lasted nearly forty years. After 1835, the Pacific became the chief scene of whaling operations. In 1820, 35,000 tons of whale oil were brought to port, by 1858 the total was 198,000. One voyage of a whaling ship lasted three or four years and was full of hard, dangerous work which could be very profitable. New England and New York provided the ports for the whalers—with New Bedford, Massachusetts, the home port for more vessels than any other.

10   *Labor and Agriculture*

As INDUSTRY grew, so did the labor force, and as it grew, labor organized—scoring some gains and dabbling in politics and in the reform movement. Spurred by the growing urban market for food and by the availability of fertile land at low prices, agricultural production increased vastly as new acreage was put under cultivation, especially in the Old Northwest.

Labor organizations, some of which were formed earlier than 1825, increased in numbers and strength until the Panic of 1837 nearly wiped them out. The unions of the time were chiefly organizations of skilled mechanics and artisans, not factory workers. Their growth was stimulated in the early 1830's by a rise in the cost of living, estimated to have been as much as 66 per cent in the two years from 1834 to 1836. As the number of unions grew, they combined to set up central labor councils within cities. The first was the Mechanics Union of Trade Associations, established in Philadelphia in 1827, and by 1836 thirteen cities had central councils. The first attempt at a national organization was made in 1834 when the National Trades' Union was formed in New York. This group held conventions each year, debated labor issues and decided not to go into politics. The Union claimed that its affiliated groups included 300,000 members in all. The economic collapse of 1837 put an end to this national organization and other unions suffered. As unemployment rose, workers no longer could or cared to continue their membership.

The unions called strikes fairly often and at least 168 strikes took place between 1833 and 1837. The carpenters in Philadelphia struck for a ten-hour day in 1827. They were supported by other unions and this strike led to the formation of the central city organization. Among the early strikes of factory workers was one that took place in Paterson, New Jersey, in 1828. The strikers were mostly children.

Many people, including the employers, held that unions were illegal conspiracies. When a union of shoemakers in Geneva, New York, went on strike in 1835 for higher wages, the presiding judge in the case of *People* v. *Fisher* declared the workers were injuring the public because "a conspiracy for such an object is against the spirit of the common law." A society of journeymen tailors suffered the same fate in New York City in 1836, although in two other cases the unions were acquitted. A notable law suit that resulted in a clear triumph for the workers took place in Boston in 1840. Members of the Bootmakers' Society were tried for attempting to force their employers to hire only union members. The court convicted them, but on an appeal to a higher court in 1841, the verdict was reversed. In a ruling that influenced other judges, Chief Justice Lemuel Shaw (1781–1861) of the Supreme Judicial Court of Massachusetts held that the common law concerning conspiracy did not apply to labor unions and that to strike for a closed shop was legal.

Organized labor entered politics in 1828 when unions in Philadelphia endorsed candidates for the city council and won several seats for candidates who were also backed by other parties. The movement spread, and within the next five years parties were formed in fifteen states, as far west as Ohio. Sixty-eight journals supported the labor movement in the early 1830's. As time went on, the labor movement, especially that part that took up political action, became more involved in reform movements than in purely labor issues. The first meeting of the New England Workingmen's Association in 1844 was attended by more reformers than labor leaders.

The Workingmen's party of New York City, organized in 1829 by unemployed artisans, placed the abolition of imprisonment for debt at the head of its list of issues. In the election that year the party polled 6,000 votes out of a total of 21,000, and elected one of its members, a carpenter, to the state Assembly. Among the party's leaders were George Henry Evans (1805–56), Robert Dale Owen (1801–77) and Frances Wright (1795–1852). All were born in England and were more interested in general social reform than in the labor movement as such.

Evans, although he worked with Owen and Miss Wright, was less radical than they. He established the first important labor journal in the United States, the *Working Man's Advocate*, in 1829. His greatest interest was in agrarianism and he agitated for cheap or free farmland to drain labor from the East and thus keep wages high. His slogan was: "Vote yourself a farm." Owen was the son of a well-known reformer, Robert Owen, and participated with his father in an experiment in socialistic living at New Harmony, Indiana. He and Miss Wright established the *Free Enquirer* in 1829 in New York. This paper advocated several reforms then without wide backing, such as freedom of thought in religion, and birth control. Miss Wright was criticized for the radical ideas she advocated and on the grounds that it was not proper for a woman to become involved in such activities as the labor movement.

When reformers such as these took over the leadership of the Workingmen's party, many members left and joined the Jacksonian Democrats, where they constituted the radical wing. They acquired the name Locofocos at a stormy meeting of Tammany Hall, the New York Democratic organization in 1835. When the more radical elements began to get the upper hand, someone turned off the gas lights. The Locofocos continued the meeting with candles which they lit with a new-style self-igniting match called locofoco. The Locofocos stood for hard money and free trade, and they distrusted banks and corporations.

Although the labor unions made some gains for their members, working conditions were not favorable. Wages were low and an unskilled laborer usually received less than $1 a day. Men factory workers were paid about $5 a week, women $1.75 to $2, and children from $1 to $2. As more machinery was introduced, less skill was required and wages went down. Between 1835 and 1845, the pay of hatters decreased from $12 to $8 a week. In addition, as immigration increased, wages of unskilled workers were driven down when the newcomers anxiously sought jobs at almost any wage. But the cost of living was low. A man could secure room and board for a week for from $1.75 to $2, a woman for $1.25 to $1.50.

The hours of labor were long and the unions were more persistent in agitating for the ten-hour day than for any other reform. By the 1830's artisans and mechanics had for the most part won the battle, but factory workers were still toiling twelve hours, or even more, per day. In 1840 the average workday was estimated at 11.4 hours. That year President Van Buren proclaimed a ten-hour day, with no loss in pay, for Federal workers. New Hampshire in 1847 was the first state to pass a law setting ten hours as the standard, and others followed. Many workers wanted shorter hours so they would have time to seek further education or otherwise improve themselves. Employers claimed more time off would lead to vice. One newspaper commented: "To be idle several of the most useful hours of the morning and evening will surely lead to intemperance and ruin."

Women were paid less than men, although their hours were little if any shorter, and they were usually the first to be laid off. A woman who wanted to work had little choice except to be a "hired girl," that is, a domestic servant, or a mill hand in a factory. A comparatively small number of women held more skilled jobs and they formed trade societies, such as the United Seamstresses Society of Baltimore and, in New York, the Ladies' Shoebinders and the Female Bookbinders. Child labor was widely used, particularly in the textile mills. Sometimes all members of a family labored in the same factory and children worked the same long hours as adults, leaving almost no time for education, let alone recreation. The states passed laws to protect child workers, but they were seldom enforced. Of the workers in Massachusetts mills in 1832, 21 per cent were children and, in Rhode Island, 41 per cent.

Overall, labor's progress from 1825 to 1850 was not impressive. The ten-hour day and the abolition of imprisonment for debt were, for the most part, achieved. However, organized labor was not very strong in 1850 and the leaders felt, probably rightly, that manufacturing and banking interests had gained in power in relation to labor. Partly to offset this, labor turned to politics, achieved little success on its own and sided more and more with the Democratic party.

Although industry and the urban labor force grew, agriculture continued to be the main business of the country and the occupation of more Americans than any other. New England could no longer compete with the West in producing grains and meat, and was turning to truck and dairy farming. The Old Northwest became the center of agricultural production in the North, while southern agriculture spread southwest and across the Mississippi. The prairies of Indiana, Illinois and Iowa baffled settlers from the East at first. For a time it was thought the land was not fertile. This was not so but problems did exist: there was little natural drainage, not enough timber, and the ordinary plow would not work in the soil, entangled as it was with the roots of the grasses that grew there.

Cotton was the biggest and most valuable non-food crop, and the South produced about seven-eighths of the world supply. The average production for the five years ending 1825 was 209,000,000 pounds; for the 1840–45 period, 822,900,000 pounds; and by 1850 production passed the 1,000,000,000 pound mark. The leading cotton-producing states in 1850 were, Alabama, Georgia, Mississippi and South Carolina. The great growth in production was caused by the expansion of the region in which cotton was grown, especially the Alabama-Mississippi area. Population in those states increased from 445,000 in 1830 to 1,377,000 in 1850. Of the latter number, 47 per cent were slaves. It was estimated that 2,500,000 of the 3,200,000 slaves in the country were employed in agriculture, and that more than 70 per cent of these were working in the cotton fields.

Cotton prices were set on the world market, so the American grower was at the mercy of many forces. In general, cotton prices went down, chiefly because of the large amount grown, while production costs went up. From 1820 to 1825, the average price per pound was 16.2 cents; in 1831–35, 7.7 cents; and there were times in 1842 and 1844 when the price dipped below 5 cents.

Wheat was grown everywhere, but the largest areas of cultivation moved steadily westward until by the 1840's wheat production in Iowa and Nebraska was significant. Wheat was a good cash crop but until canals and railroads were available it was hard to get it to market cheaply because of its bulk and weight. The United States produced 84,823,000 bushels in 1839 and 100,485,000 bushels in 1849. Many grist mills were required to turn the wheat into flour and there were 4,354 in 1840. The larger mills were found in Baltimore, Buffalo and Rochester.

Corn was the most widespread crop of all. It was the first crop a pioneer in the West planted, since it grew with little care and provided products that fed the farmer's family and the livestock. It was cheaper than wheat, and slave diets included large amounts of corn. In the South, 18,000,000 acres were planted in 1849, more than three times as many acres as were devoted to cotton. The nation produced 317,531,000 bushels of corn in 1839; 592,071,000 in 1849.

The potato, a vegetable of the western hemisphere, was grown mostly in the northern states. In 1839, New England produced over thirty-five million bushels, about one-third of the entire American crop. New York State grew 30,123,000 bushels. The potato blight greatly reduced production in 1843 and the situation was even worse in 1844 and 1845.

Sugar production was concentrated in southern Louisiana where growers turned out 110 million pounds in 1828 and 205 million in

1844. The maximum number of plantations, 1,536, was reached in 1849. Sugar cane was a difficult and expensive crop to produce, requiring an enormous amount of labor and more than 100,000 slaves were engaged in sugar production in 1849. The production of rice, like sugar, was confined to a small area—in this case the coastal regions of Georgia and South Carolina. Rice required more slaves per unit of production than any other crop because of the complicated procedures that had to be followed. The United States produced 215 million pounds of rice in 1849, but the size of the crop was declining.

Tobacco, another plant native to America, was a valuable crop in colonial times and its cultivation continued on a large scale, although in relative terms tobacco was less important to the agricultural south than it had been. The average value per acre was high, and encouraged wasteful methods of cultivation which exhausted the soil in about four years. Most of the tobacco was used domestically, unlike colonial times when most of it was exported, and plug tobacco for chewing accounted for a large part of the crop. Hemp, which was used in making bags and rope, was produced in central Kentucky on 3,520 plantations.

Farmers, especially those on the frontier who were busy creating farms, often neglected the feeding and breeding of their livestock. By contrast, from time to time great interest was shown in importing purebred animals to improve domestic stock. The Old Northwest supplied the East with beef, most of it driven to market until the railroad made transportation easier and faster. From Texas, cattle were driven to New Orleans beginning in 1842, and 1,000 head of cattle were driven all the way from Texas to Ohio in 1846. Some livestock was slaughtered in the West and the preserved products shipped east. Cincinnati, Ohio, by 1850 was packing 27 per cent of the West's meat products. The census of 1850 showed the nation had 6,485,094 milch cows; 1,700,741 oxen; and 10,293,069 "other" or beef cattle. Milk could not be marketed very far from the farm until in the

1840's the railroad made it possible to enlarge the milk shed for the benefit of urban residents.

Pork from hogs was important in the American diet, especially in the South. Cincinnati was sometimes called "Porkopolis" because of the amount of pork packed there. Sheep, too, were raised on many farms, mostly for their wool. New England was the area of most sheep raising, with flocks expanding until the 1840's because the price of raw wool was high. One Vermont county reported 373 sheep to the square mile.

Farming in the first half of the nineteenth century required a great deal of hard labor. The farmer's first source of labor was himself and his family. Children learned chores as soon as they were big enough. In addition, there were many farm laborers—"hired hands" as they were commonly called. A hired hand in 1828 received about $8 a month and room and board. The rate went up slowly over the years. A Yankee farmer in 1835 paid $10 to $12 a month, and ten years later in New England hired hands received $12 to $15 a month, while in Iowa and northern Illinois wages were up to $20.

With labor scarce, with plenty of land to bring under cultivation and with a growing urban population to be fed, a strong incentive existed to invent farm machinery that would enable a farmer to plant more land and raise larger crops. The improvement of the plow and the invention of the reaper were the most important advances in farm technology. John Deere (1804–86), a Vermont blacksmith by trade, introduced the steel plow in 1837. With the use of steel, soil would not stick to the mouldboard—the part that turns the soil over. Deere later established a plant in Moline, Illinois, which manufactured thousands of plows and other agricultural machinery.

Cutting grain by hand was hard slow work; an expert could cut no more than four acres a day. Large-scale grain production was made possible when Cyrus H. McCormick (1809–84) invented a mechanical reaper in 1831. He built a factory in Chicago in 1847 and turned out reapers by the hundreds. McCormick sold them to farmers for $120, with $30 down and six months to pay the rest. A further step in speeding up farm work was the invention of a workable horse-powered thresher-cleaner in the late 1830's.

Jesse Buel (1778–1839) and Edmund Ruffin (1794–1865) improved agricultural practice by their experiments and their advocacy of scientific methods. Buel was born in Connecticut, became a newspaper editor and in 1834 founded the *Cultivator*—the most popular farm journal of its day. Buel established a model farm, which became quite profitable, where he demonstrated the value of crop rotation, drainage, deep plowing and heavy manuring. Ruffin, born in Virginia, was an extreme proslavery man who advocated secession of the South. As an agriculturalist he was a pioneer in soil chemistry, endeavoring to restore the fertility of the soil in Virginia. He advocated the use of marl, and proved his point by restoring worn-out tobacco land. He, like Buel, established a popular farm magazine, the *Farmers' Register* in 1833.

Of the 5,420,000 Americans gainfully employed in 1840, 3,721,000 were in agriculture. Farming was of primary economic importance, and the belief also persisted that it was a superior way of life. Many felt, as Buel wrote, that

> There is no business of life which so highly conduces to the prosperity of a nation, and to the happiness of its entire population, as that of cultivating the soil.

11 Transportation, Communication and Technology

INDUSTRY AND agriculture might produce more manufactured goods and larger crops, but without improvements in transportation they were of little value. Transportation was the major economic problem of the nineteenth century. No matter how much roads were improved, the speed of movement and the weight of goods that could be transported were limited to the ability of horses and oxen. Canals made it possible to move heavy, bulky freight cheaply, but the pace was still slow. To the advantages of the canal, the railroad added speed. Finally, the telegraph made it possible to plan, direct and control the movement of freight trains, as well as to disseminate national, business and personal news speedily.

Road building continued after canals and railroads entered the picture, but there was not the urgency about it that caused Congress as early as 1806 to approve the first federally financed project, the National Road. With construction delayed by the War of 1812, the road did not reach Wheeling, Virginia, from Cumberland, Maryland, until 1818. After 1825 it was continued westward, reaching Columbus, Ohio, in 1833. It was extended to Vandalia, Illinois, by 1850, but only the part to Springfield, Ohio, was fully surfaced. Turnpike construction began early in the century and passed its peak by 1825. Turnpikes were toll roads, usually constructed by private companies. Most were in the northeast, and Pennsylvania, for example, reached its maximum mileage in 1832 with 2,400 miles of toll roads. Roads in general were poorly constructed and poorly maintained.

The second quarter of the nineteenth century was the era of canal building in the United States. The inspiration came from the canal building in Great Britain that was started in the second half of the eighteenth century. The canals at first were more important for transporting agricultural products than manufactured goods. Another incentive to canal building was the desire of eastern business interests to direct the flow of western products to the East rather than down the Mississippi to New Orleans.

The most successful canal and the one that triggered the boom in canal building in the United States was the Erie Canal, which was begun in 1817 and completed in 1825. Its energetic sponsor was De Witt Clinton (1769–1828) who at various times was a senator, mayor of New York City and governor of the state from 1817 to 1821. The completed canal ran 363 miles from the Hudson River near Albany to Lake Erie at Buffalo. It was forty feet wide at the top, twenty-eight at the bottom and four deep. It had eighty-three locks to raise and lower boats and cost $7,000,000 to build.

The Erie Canal was an instant success. By way of the Great Lakes and the canal, farmers in the Old Northwest could ship their products at costs low enough to secure a market in the East. Within fifteen years of its opening, wheat and flour equal to 1,000,000 barrels of flour moved east on the canal in one year. Eastern manufacturers were equally enthusiastic. By 1836 they sent $10,000,000 worth of goods westward. Passenger travel was also heavy and the canal became a favorite route for immigrants going to pioneer in the West. Cargo boats sold deck passage, but the traveler had to bring his own food. Passenger boats made only about four miles an hour, which was slower than a first-rate stagecoach, but they were safer, smoother and cheaper. The canal stimulated the growth of cities along the way, such as Rochester, Utica and Syracuse.

The success of the Erie Canal caused other states to build canals.

In the East, canals were constructed to compete with the Erie for the trade of the West. The Pennsylvania Canal, from Philadelphia to Pittsburgh, was completed in 1834. It was even longer than the Erie—394 miles—and at one point cable cars carried the boats over the backbone of the Alleghenies. Work on the Chesapeake and Ohio Canal began at Washington, D. C., in 1828, and it was built as far as Cumberland, Maryland, but not on to the Ohio River as planned. Other canals in the East were built to connect inland areas with tidewater, and to improve shipping along the coast from north to south.

The midwest was the other area in which canal building was undertaken on a large scale. The Ohio and Erie Canal, completed in 1833, connected the Ohio River with Lake Erie, from Portsmouth to Cleveland on the lake. The Miami and Erie was built in the western part of the state, from Cincinnati to Toledo, and was completed in 1845. The Wabash and Erie Canal in Indiana, finished in 1843, also connected Lake Erie with the Ohio River.

The canal era was a short-lived one because of the development of railroads in the 1840's. By 1850 some canals were being abandoned. Total canal mileage increased from 1,270 in 1830 to 3,700 in 1850. By that time about $125,000,000 had been spent on canals and, since most were constructed with public funds, some states had gone heavily in debt.

The first American railroad in the modern sense of the term was the Baltimore and Ohio, with its starting point in Baltimore. The first spade of earth for its construction was turned on July 4, 1828. Thirteen miles of track were built by 1830 and service started. Horsepower was used at first, except for some experimental runs by Peter Cooper's locomotive, *Tom Thumb*. By 1831, though, a satisfactory steam locomotive was in use.

An early attempt to use steam power took place in 1829 on what became the Delaware and Hudson Railroad, using a nine-horsepower locomotive imported from England and called the *Stourbridge Lion*. It was too heavy for the rails and its use was abandoned. The South Carolina Canal and Railroad opened on Christmas Day, 1830. With a steam locomotive built in the United States and named the *Best Friend of Charleston*, the first scheduled run on a steam-powered railroad left Charleston with 141 passengers. By fall of 1833, this road was 136 miles long, the longest continuous railroad in the world. Another early railroad was the Mohawk and Hudson which began service in August, 1831, between Albany and Schenectady, New York, a distance of seventeen miles.

Railroad construction went on at such a pace that by 1840 there were 3,000 miles of track and ten years later, 9,000. Every state east of the Mississippi had some trackage, but more than half the total was in New England and the Middle Atlantic states. Atlanta, Georgia, was becoming the railroad center of the southeast, while in the Old Northwest, Ohio had more miles of road than any other state. With many different companies building railroads with short mileage, the problem of traveling long distances was complicated. At one time there were seven different lines between Albany and Buffalo. A passenger could not buy a through ticket, had to change trains and stations at each point, and the schedules of the different roads were not coordinated. The Erie Railroad in the southern part of the state gave New York a through route across the state. Running from Piermont near New York City to Dunkirk on Lake Erie, it was completed in 1851 and with 483 miles of tracks was the longest road in the world. The Illinois Central Railroad, running south from Chicago for 700 miles, in 1850 was the first to be aided by a grant of public land from Congress, receiving 2,500,000 acres. The road was completed in 1856.

In the early days of railroading, travel was neither very safe nor very comfortable. The first passenger coaches copied the stagecoach, even to providing an elevated seat for the coachman. These were soon replaced by corridor-type coaches. The first freight cars had no roofs, but in a few years they looked much like modern freight cars except smaller. The first rails were long strips of iron fastened to wooden rails, with a tendency to come loose, curl and thrust themselves up through the floor of the car. At first the rails were fastened to granite blocks, but in the 1840's wooden cross ties began to be used.

The locomotive, which began as a steam engine mounted on wheels, developed a look of its own as well as more power. Swivel wheels under the front of the locomotive let it navigate curves more easily, while the cowcatcher insured that more damage would be done to the cow than the locomotive. Cabs were added to protect the engineer, especially in the North where one of the railroad's advantages over canal and river transportation was that it could be operated all winter. The gauge—the distance between the rails—varied from road to road. This made the interchange of equipment impossible and it was many years before a standard gauge—four feet, eight and one half inches—was settled upon. Passenger fares were two and a half cents a mile in some parts of the country, and up to five cents in other areas.

The art of building and running railroads called for new skills. Among the pioneer railroaders were Matthias W. Baldwin (1795–1866) and John B. Jervis (1795–1885). Baldwin, a New Jersey-born industrialist and philanthropist, built one of the first successful locomotives in America, *Old Ironsides*, in 1832 and it ran for twenty years. Two years later he established the Baldwin Locomotive Works which by 1836 produced forty locomotives in a year. Jervis was a civil engineer who helped build the Erie Canal and the Delaware and Hudson Canal. In 1832 he designed and constructed the locomotive *Experiment*, which was the fastest then built. Jervis became chief engineer of the Croton Aqueduct, planned to provide water for New York City, in 1836.

Between 1825 and 1850 the nation's transportation system moved through a short age of canals to the establishment of the age of the railroad. More goods were carried by water than by rail, but the future clearly belonged to the railroad. The railroad system handled most of the passenger traffic because of its greater speed, but already

there was criticism of the railroad for what it did to the landscape.
Daniel Webster, though no enemy of industrialism, observed in 1847
that

> railroad directors and railroad projectors are no enthusiastic lovers of
> landscape beauty; a handsome field or lawn, beautiful copses, and all
> the gorgeousness of forest scenery, pass for little in their eyes. Their
> business is to cut and slash, to level or deface a finely rounded field, and
> fill up beautifully winding valleys.

The invention and development of the steamboat in the first
quarter of the century made possible the early expansion of American
economic life. Inland waterways, the Ohio and Mississippi rivers
especially, were prosperous arteries for trade. The use of steamboats to
carry freight grew in the 1825–50 period in spite of canals and
railroads. Many canals, in fact, fed lake or ocean shipping. About 200
steamboats were operating on the Ohio and Mississippi by 1830, and
within a dozen years their tonnage exceeded that of all the ships of
Great Britain. The *J. M. White* was claimed as the fastest boat on the
Mississippi in 1844, making the run upriver from New Orleans to St.
Louis in three days and twenty-three hours. Shipping on the Great
Lakes increased every year, and in 1850 Cleveland was the leading
port. The future importance of Chicago was foretold by the 300 vessels
that docked there in 1833.

Boats on the Mississippi, the Hudson and on the coastal runs
grew larger and more luxurious. Some were 300 feet long. The
Massachusetts, on the New York to Providence route, had a dining
salon 160 feet long, that could seat 175 people and became a men's
cabin at night. The river boats had many accidents, most the result of
boiler explosions. When this happened to the *Oronoko* on the Mississippi in 1838, 130 or more died. Federal safety inspection began the
same year.

The advent of steam-powered oceangoing vessels marked the
further progress of the steamship. The *Savannah* crossed the Atlantic in

1819 using steam power for a small part of the voyage, but it was 1838 before all-steam crossings began. In that year, two British ships, the *Sirius* and the *Great Western*, inaugurated service from England to America. The *Great Western* crossed in fifteen days—two and a half days less than the *Sirius*. Such oceangoing ships did not prosper for some years, however. Fuel for the engines occupied more space than the cargo, salt water corroded boilers and the engines themselves were difficult to arrange satisfactorily, given the roughness of the ocean compared with inland waters. Ocean travel on steamships came into its own after 1848. An American-built ship, the *Atlantic*, that sailed from New York in April, 1850, made better time by one day than the British Cunard Line ships. The steamship and the railroad revolutionized travel and transportation and in this period the transportation pattern for the rest of the century was set.

Until the mid-1840's, the transmission of news, or information of any kind, was limited by the speed of the fastest means of transportation. For some years people in several countries had considered the possibility of using electric power to transmit signals over wires. Samuel F. B. Morse (1791–1872), who was born in Massachusetts, pursued the idea. He began his career as a painter and achieved considerable success, but about 1837 he gave up painting to attempt to develop a telegraph. He used electrical power to transmit short and long impulses (dots and dashes) over a wire. With combinations of the dots and dashes standing for letters of the alphabet, messages of any kind could be sent easily and quickly.

Congress voted $30,000 for the construction of an experimental line between Washington and Baltimore, and on May 24, 1844, Morse demonstrated the practicality of the telegraph by sending a message, "What hath God wrought," from the capital. Morse thought the government should own the telegraph, but Congress decided otherwise and in 1846 the original line became private property. Morse owed a great deal to the assistance he received from Alfred Vail (1807–59) and Ezra Cornell (1807–74). As Morse's partner, Vail provided funds and made improvements in the telegraph instrument and in the Morse code. Cornell, who started life as a laborer and made a fortune in business, provided money and supervised building the first telegraph line. He devised a method for stringing the wire on poles and promoted the extension of telegraph lines after 1844. Cornell was the principal founder of Cornell University.

The telegraph network spread rapidly. By fall of 1846 the cities on the Washington-Boston route were linked up. The next year lines extended to Pittsburgh, Cincinnati and Louisville, and by 1848 every state east of the Mississippi except Florida was connected by wire. The telegraph rendered valuable service during the Mexican War and President Polk's message to Congress in December, 1848, was transmitted as far west as St. Louis. Newspapers and business firms also made regular use of the telegraph.

The scope and services of the United States Post Office also expanded, with 8,401 offices and 115,000 miles of routes as early as 1830. Mail began moving by railroad in 1838, and two years later clerks were sorting mail on moving trains. An overland mail service to California was inaugurated in 1849. The use of the mails was stimulated in 1845 when rates were reduced so that a letter could be sent for five cents for distances up to 300 miles, and for ten cents over longer distances. Postage stamps were introduced in 1847.

Among the services that improved transportation and communication were the express companies, the first of which was established in 1839 by William Francis Harnden to operate between New York City and Boston. Express service provided fast and safe transportation of small packages, valuable papers and money. Alvin Adams founded a rival firm and by 1843 his business extended south and west to New Orleans and St. Louis. The best-known names associated with the express business are those of Henry Wells (1805–78) and William G. Fargo (1818–81). After working for other expressmen, Wells in 1843 established a service between New York City and Buffalo. The next year he joined with Fargo to form Wells Fargo and Company, which soon was doing business as far west as Chicago and St. Louis. Five years later this company merged with others to form the American Express Company, after which the two men moved to San Francisco. Their new organization became famous as the company that carried the mail and the gold dust of the Forty-Niners.

The increase in the number of inventions was one sign of the speed of change: from 1790 to 1811 about 77 patents were issued a year, by 1830 the number reached 544, and for the next decade averaged about 650 a year. The number of steam engines in use also pointed up the change: the secretary of the treasury reported in 1838 that 3,010 such machines were in operation, of which 800 were on steamboats, 350 in locomotives and 1,860 in manufacturing plants and public works.

Rubber interested many inventors, and for years inventors attempted to make its use practical. The chief difficulty was that it melted too easily when subjected to heat. The problem was solved by an American, Charles Goodyear (1800–60), who spent several years seeking a solution. At one point Goodyear was jailed for debt, and he is said to have sold his children's textbooks to raise money. Finally, in 1839, he accidently dropped some rubber that had been mixed with sulphur on a hot stove. "Vulcanizing," which gives rubber strength, elasticity and the ability to resist heat and cold, had been developed, and rubber could be used in a variety of products. Goodyear collected royalties, but became involved in litigation over patents and died poor.

The invention of the sewing machine made mass production of clothing possible, and home sewing faster and easier. Elias Howe (1819–67) exhibited his first sewing machine in 1845, and patented another in 1846. Isaac Merritt Singer (1811–75) also patented a sewing machine in 1851. Howe sued for infringement of his patent and Singer lost, but the latter already had a going manufacturing concern so the men joined forces and both became rich.

The dissemination of more printed information faster, particularly in the case of newspapers, owed much to Richard Marsh Hoe (1812–86). Hoe went to work in his father's business, where printing presses were manufactured, when he was fifteen. He designed the rotary press, in which type could be fastened to a large central cylinder, in 1846–47. It quadrupled the speed of printing and turned out 8,000 papers an hour when used by the Philadelphia *Public Ledger* for the first time in 1847.

Photography can be dated from 1839, when Louis J. M. Daguerre, a Frenchman, demonstrated his "daguerretype." The process was at once taken up in the United States and one of its early practitioners and improvers was John W. Draper (1811–82). Draper was appointed professor of chemistry at New York University in 1838. He was probably the first American to use Daguerre's process, and in 1840 he took what is generally considered to be the first satisfactory portrait of an individual. The first photographic studio was opened in New York in 1840.

The many changes in industry, commerce, labor, agriculture, transportation, communication and technology from 1825 to 1850 were not only impressive and beneficial to the nation, but also, when compared with the previous quarter century, showed that the pace of industrialism—and of American life in general—was speeding up.

12   The Blacks: Slave and Free

THE QUARTER century from 1825 to 1850 was a crucial one in the history of slavery and the blacks in the United States. Negro slavery became so imbedded in the life of the South that even some of those who were against it saw no practical way of ridding the nation of it. Active and violent opposition to slavery appeared in the North, and in reaction, slavery was defended in the South, as a necessity, even as a positive good. The split between North and South, which had been temporarily closed by the Compromise of 1820, was opened wider than ever and threatened to break the Union in two.

The black population, both slave and free, grew considerably. The 1830 census showed 2,328,642 blacks, of whom 2,009,043 were slaves and 319,599 were free. In all, the blacks were 18.1 per cent of the nation's population. This census also showed that 3,777 Negroes who were heads of families owned slaves; that 750 free blacks in New Orleans owned slaves; that one of these owned 32. By 1840, the black population was 2,873,648, constituting 16.1 per cent of the total population. There were now 2,487,355 slaves and 386,293 free blacks. Ohio, for example, had 17,342 blacks; the city of Boston, 2,427. The 1850 census counted 3,638,808 blacks and showed a further decline as a part of the whole population, to 15.7 per cent. There were 3,204,313 slaves and 434,495 free Negroes. It was estimated that of the slaves, 2,800,000 lived on farms and plantations while 400,000 lived in cities and towns. More slaves were counted in Virginia than any other state—472,528. South Carolina followed with 384,984 and Georgia with 381,682.

The extensive cotton plantation with a large number of slaves fixed the image of the South, but the plantation system by no means constituted the whole South. In North Carolina, for example, two-thirds of the farms consisted of less than 100 acres—500 being the minimum for a plantation. Such farms were owned and operated by yeoman farmers who, along with mechanics, storekeepers and the owners of small plantations, constituted the middle class of the South. The yeoman farmer worked his own land, and might own a few slaves or none. Poor whites made up another class which scratched out a living on soil abandoned by planters or in the infertile hill areas. The 1850 census showed that of the white population of the South, 76 per cent were yeoman farmers who owned no slaves. In all, 347,525 southerners held slaves, but only 11 owned 500 or more; 254 owned 200 or more; and about 8,000 owned 50 or more. Three-quarters of the slaves were owned by only 7 per cent of the whites.

The South was dominated by the owners of cotton, rice and sugar plantations, together with the professional class. A plantation was large but its size was restricted by the distance it was practical for the slaves to walk from their quarters to the fields. Planters who owned thousands of acres usually had several different plantations and were absentee owners of most of them, turning up perhaps only once a year for an inspection. Wade Hampton III, for instance, owned six plantations in Mississippi, totalling 10,409 acres with 900 slaves. A planter often professed to disdain money matters and yet he owned a very complicated economic unit which was sometimes precariously balanced between profit and loss. The voices of the planters, and of the lawyers allied with the planters, were the voices the nation heard in Congress and elsewhere, speaking for the whole South.

While defenders of slavery claimed that the Negro was happy in bondage, southerners lived in fear of slave revolts. An insurrection erupted in Southampton County, Virginia, in the summer of 1831. It was led by Nat Turner (1800–31), a slave who was somewhat of a mystic and who believed he had been chosen to lead his people out of slavery. He and twenty or thirty followers killed his master and the family, then went after others. Sixty whites were murdered within twenty-four hours. Just as it appeared the revolt would spread, militia and Federal troops attacked the blacks, killing more than a hundred. Others, including three free Negroes, were seized and hanged. Turner was captured after about six weeks and was hanged on November 11. The panicky South retaliated by tightening the Black Codes—the state laws that regulated the conduct of slaves—and by attacks on the northern abolitionists, whom they blamed for inciting the slaves.

The last occasion, it now appears, on which the South itself might have begun to end slavery was a debate over emancipation in the Virginia legislature in 1831–32. This debate was caused by the furor over Turner's rebellion. The younger legislators from western Virginia were generally in favor of abolishing slavery, while the eastern tidewater area's representatives were mainly members of, or spoke for, the planter class. On the crucial ballot on a resolution that would instruct the legislature to enact an abolition law, the vote was strongly against the proposal. This was the last time any southern legislative body gave any consideration to emancipating the slaves.

Whether the system of raising cotton with slave labor was a sound one from the viewpoint of business and economics has long been debated. Leaving out the moral and humanitarian aspects of slavery, did the slave owners profit more or less than they would have with free labor? Was the South as a whole better or worse off economically? The planter had to make a sizable capital investment in slaves. A good field hand cost about $800 in 1830, and prices reached a high point in 1837 of $1,300 in the deep South. After the panic of that year, prices tumbled, but by 1850 were back to $1,200. The owner also had to feed, clothe and house the slaves and take care of them in illness and old age. One estimate is that this cost about $135 a year, not a small sum in those days.

In return, the owners had the labor of the blacks to do with as they would. Most of the work required little skill and few tools, and large numbers of slaves could be used at a time under comparatively little supervision. On the other hand, the black's condition as a slave did not encourage initiative. Some plantation owners certainly made a great deal of money; others went bankrupt or were often on the verge of it. But profit or loss did not depend entirely on slavery. They resulted from good or bad weather, efficient or inefficient management, and the price of cotton. Whether the individual owners and the South as a whole would have been better off economically with a system of free labor, as in the North, seems impossible to prove.

Basically, the slaves' work was unpleasant because they had no control over it. As field hands, they worked long hours, often under a hot sun. White overseers and black "drivers," the latter responsible for a group of fellow slaves under the owner or overseer, were under pressure to produce results. The slave who lagged could be punished in any way the owner or overseer wished, and whipping was the most common method. House servants, or slaves who were taught skills such as carpentry, were better off. On some plantations slaves were treated kindly, on others life was harsh and punishment frequent. At its best, the slave system was paternalistic and implied that the black slaves were inferior creatures, stupid, lazy and sometimes comic. The system denied the fundamental humanity of the black slaves, more because of their color than because of their servitude.

Slaves who lived in cities generally fared better than their country counterparts. Most city slaves were in domestic service, but a number were carpenters, barbers, painters or followed other trades. More of the carpenters in Charleston, South Carolina, in 1848 were black than white. City slaves worked in factories and in some cases were owned by the corporation that ran the plant. Most of the tobacco processors in Richmond, Virginia, were slaves, and in the 1840's an iron works there replaced its white workmen with black slaves. The firemen of Savannah, Georgia, were slaves. Sometimes slaves were hired out by their masters to perform skilled or unskilled labor. Such slaves were often allowed to keep some of their earnings, and they might save enough to purchase their freedom. A few free Negroes became successful businessmen. One in Charleston operated a first-class hotel that was patronized by whites. Another became a rich merchant in Macon, Georgia, who entertained his white friends at dinner but refrained from sitting at table with them.

Plantation slaves lived in rude cabins and wore plain, coarse clothing. Some of the dresses, trousers and shirts were homespun, others were bought from the North or Great Britain and were made from cheap material known as "Negro cloth." The usual food ration for a slave was a peck of corn meal a week and three or four pounds of salt pork or bacon. Fresh meat was seldom issued, but some slaves were allowed to raise their own vegetables and chickens. Family life of a sort existed, but was at best difficult. The law did not recognize the legality of marriage between slaves. Some masters encouraged settled family arrangements and insisted on wedding ceremonies. Others did not care what happened as long as no word of trouble reached their ears. Since each slave was an individual piece of property, a master could sell a husband while keeping the wife, or separate a parent from children. Some owners went out of their way to keep families together; others, out of economic pressure or simple callousness, made no attempt to maintain family units. Marriages between whites and blacks were prohibited, but this did not prevent a good deal of miscegenation, mostly between white men and black women. By 1850 the census showed that mulattoes, men and women of mixed blood, amounted to a little more than 11 per cent of the total black population, or around 375,000 persons.

The slaves' social life was restricted, but there were times, such as Christmas, when it was customary to allow time off from work and to provide extra food and drink, and dancing. On both social and religious occasions, slaves expressed themselves in song which by now was a combination of native African rhythms and the hymns of

American Protestantism. Many slaves became Christians and religious observance was encouraged. As time went on, though, the gathering of blacks alone with a Negro preacher was frowned upon because it gave the slaves an opportunity to plot against their masters. The opportunity for formal education was nonexistent. In fact, the laws of the southern states generally forbade teaching slaves to read and write. These laws, however, were seldom strictly enforced and some slaves learned a bit of reading and writing from their masters or mistresses or their children.

After January 1, 1808, it was illegal to import slaves into the United States. With this source of supply largely cut off, and with the increase in the acreage devoted to cotton, the domestic slave trade became a big business in itself. The demand for more slaves came from the deep South and the Southwest while the upper South—Virginia in particular—found itself with a surplus of slaves. Professional slave-traders appeared, and though they were looked down on by the slave owners who dealt with them, they were an important factor in the economy of the South. Washington was notorious as a center of the slave trade, although it was not the largest market, because many people found it difficult to face the fact that human beings were sold like cattle in the capital of the world's most democratic nation. The firm of Franklin and Armfield operated here and owned a large—and what they termed a model—stockade in Alexandria, then a part of the District of Columbia, where slaves were housed before being sent south by boat, or overland by foot. The firm bought and sold 1,000 to 1,200 slaves a year.

In spite of the ban on the importation of slaves, the traffic went on to some extent, aided both by southerners who wanted more slaves and by northern shipowners who were willing to smuggle slaves for a handsome profit. Perhaps as many as 250,000 slaves were brought in this way between 1808 and 1860. The British tried to stop the traffic and in 1843 the United States agreed to join Britain in patrolling the west coast of Africa. Over the next nine years, the American Navy captured nineteen slave ships.

Runaway slaves were a problem in several ways. From the standpoint of a slave owner, a runaway slave was an economic loss and even if recaptured, expenses were involved. In addition, the northern antislavery elements fought any attempt to enforce the fugitive slave law and this irritated southern opinion. The Federal fugitive slave law dated from 1793 but as antislavery sentiment grew, northern states passed "personal liberty" laws which gave alleged runaway slaves the right to a trial by jury. The issue came to a head in 1842 when the Supreme Court declared that the states could not legislate at all concerning fugitive slaves. The Court, on the other hand, also said that the states had no responsibility for enforcing the Federal law. In a few cases runaway slaves were rescued by force from their captors, while at the same time, a few northerners became professional slave catchers.

Two shipboard mutinies by slaves aroused passions on both sides of the slavery controversy. A Spanish ship, the *Amistad*, sailed from Havana in June, 1839, with fifty-four Negro slaves aboard. One, Cinqué, who was a headman in his African home, led an uprising in which the slaves killed the captain and three crew members. The other two whites were ordered to sail the ship to Africa. They misled the slaves, however, and the ship ended up off Long Island. The slave interests, led by John Forsyth, secretary of state, attempted to turn the slaves over to Spain. Abolitionists brought suit to prevent this and the case eventually reached the Supreme Court. With former President John Quincy Adams arguing forcefully on behalf of the blacks, the Court found they had been illegally kidnaped in Africa and set them free to go home. The *Creole* case began in the fall of 1841 when an American ship of that name sailed from Virginia for New Orleans with a cargo of slaves. The slaves mutinied, killed one white crew member and forced the ship to sail to Nassau in the West Indies, a

British possession where slavery was illegal. The British freed the slaves, except those who had actively participated in the mutiny. The American government demanded the return of the slaves but the British refused. In 1855 the matter was finally settled when Great Britain agreed to pay $110,000 to the United States.

As the cotton economy became dominant, slavery was defended, sometimes apologetically, as necessary economically. Toward the middle of the century, as northern attacks on slavery became stronger, southerners defended slavery as a positive good. Antislavery voices were stilled throughout the South. The proslavery argument was based on the assumption that Negroes were biologically inferior. From this it followed that they must be kept in bondage for their own good. The Bible was often cited to show that religion and the church sanctioned slavery, and more than one member of the clergy defended the institution. People such as Calhoun also argued that no civilization could advance culturally unless a slave class existed to perform the hard labor, thus freeing the upper class for higher endeavors. Calhoun went so far as to claim that slavery was "the most safe and stable basis for free institutions in the world." Proslavery advocates argued that the laboring class of the North was in the same position as black slaves in the South. Factory hands were poor and had no security, they said, whereas slaves were taken care of all their lives.

The proslavery argument was also supported by Thomas E. Dew (1802–46), a brilliant classical scholar who taught political economy at William and Mary College, of which he became president. Spurred by the 1832 debate in the Virginia legislature, Dew wrote one of the first strong defenses of slavery as part of the natural order. He argued that because of their color, black slaves could never be set free in the United States to live side by side with the whites. If slavery were abolished, all blacks would have to be deported to Africa and this, he said, was impractical.

All the southern states passed laws against the publishing of antislavery writings, or even talking against slavery. They also attempted to prevent abolitionist propaganda from coming into the South by the mails, arguing that enough blacks could read so that they would be incited to armed revolt. Some states even offered sizable rewards for the arrest or death of leading northern abolitionists.

The more than 400,000 free blacks in the United States in 1850 were about evenly divided between north and south, with more of them—about 80,000—living in Maryland than any other state. North Carolina, for example, counted 27,000 and Pennsylvania more than 53,000. These Negroes had freedom, but beyond that they were little better off than blacks in slavery. Race prejudice was strong in the North as well as in the South. The southern states restricted the movements and activities of free blacks. In Georgia it was illegal for free Negroes to be typesetters; in South Carolina they could not be clerks; and most states made it illegal for them to buy or sell liquor. They fared little better in the northern cities to which they usually brought no practical skills. Even if they did, the white unions refused them admission. And, north or south, they might be falsely charged as being escaped slaves, or even kidnaped back into slavery. By 1840 only four northern states—all in New England—allowed Negroes to vote on an equal basis with whites.

Mob violence against northern free blacks was not uncommon. Two of the worst incidents took place in Cincinnati and Philadelphia. In Cincinnati in 1829, a band of whites ran some Negroes out of the city by force and frightened others so that more than 1,000 fled, some going to Canada to settle. Three days of rioting took place in Philadelphia in 1834 when a mob of whites entered a Negro section of the city, burned homes and beat up a number of blacks. The second day they burned down a church and it was not until the third day that the police ended the violence.

Free blacks in the North found some opportunities to secure an education, although almost always in separate schools. New York City with 15,000 Negroes in 1828 had two schools; Philadelphia with 20,000 blacks had three schools. By 1835 there were six primary schools for black children in New York City with an enrollment of 925. Ohio excluded blacks from its public schools in 1829, but twenty years later established publicly supported schools. Prudence Crandall (1803–89), an educator and abolitionist, found out how strong race prejudice could be when she opened a girls' school in Canterbury, Connecticut, in 1831 and admitted one black girl. When the protests grew, she shut the school and reopened it as a school for black girls only. Mobs dumped manure in the school well and carried out other acts of vandalism. Miss Crandall was arrested under a new law that made it illegal to teach "a person of color" who was not an inhabitant of the state. She was convicted but the verdict was reversed on appeal.

As the quarter century closed, slavery appeared more entrenched in the South than ever before, while the antislavery movement in the North was growing and becoming more belligerent.

13   The Antislavery Movement

ALTHOUGH ANTISLAVERY sentiment was present in colonial days, no fervent crusade against slavery arose until the 1830's. Not all those who thought slavery an evil agreed on what should be done about it. At one extreme were the abolitionists who demanded immediate emancipation of all slaves. In the center were those who hoped the institution could be phased out gradually. At the other end of the spectrum were men and women who were personally opposed to slavery and wanted to keep it from spreading, but did not think it should be interfered with in the states where it existed.

The change from vague antislavery sentiment to active and even violent action owed its start to a wave of religious revivalism which began in western New York in 1824 and swept much of the North by 1830. The leading figure in this revival was Charles G. Finney (1792–1875), a Presbyterian minister for whom the Broadway Tabernacle was established in New York City in 1834. Finney went to Oberlin College in 1837 to teach, and in 1851 became its president. The revival Finney led emphasized social reform through religious belief and action. Good works were stressed in such fields as temperance, foreign missions, women's rights and the emancipation of the slaves. From the point of view of his followers, slavery was sinful.

The abolition of slavery in other countries was a further influence. Slavery in the British Empire, including the nearby West Indies, was abolished in 1833; while the Latin American countries, beginning with Argentina in 1813, ended the system as they won their independence. France abolished slavery in its West Indian colonies in 1848.

One of the early attempts at solving the slavery problem called for transporting the blacks to Africa. For this purpose the American Colonization Society was founded in 1817, with many leading public figures active in it and with support from slaveholders of the South as well as from northern antislavery people. Territory which became the independent state of Liberia was acquired on the west coast of Africa. At first only free Negroes were sent, but later some slaves were freed for this purpose. Results, however, were meager. The process was very expensive and few blacks cared to go. Only 1,420 blacks had been settled in Liberia by 1830, and the society in its whole career was able to transport only 12,000. Many antislavery leaders turned against the scheme in the early 1830's when it became obvious that some slaveholders were supporters because they thought the slaves were less likely to cause trouble if free blacks could be sent out of the country.

Local and state antislavery societies, including some in the southern states, were organized. One was founded in Maryland in 1825 and several groups existed in North Carolina. The New England Anti-Slavery Society came into existence in 1832 and by 1836 there were more than 500 groups, but all of them were in the North. The first national organization was formed in Philadelphia in 1833, the American Anti-Slavery Society. Free Negroes were active at this meeting and three became members of the executive committee. In 1836, however, when it was proposed that a black minister speak at the society's convention, the idea was turned down by abolitionist leaders who thought the time had not yet come to associate with Negroes that publicly. The Society was active, distributing 25,000 copies of one tract and 50,000 of another in the South in 1835. By 1838 the Society claimed 1,350 local societies affiliated with it.

The first president of the American Anti-Slavery Society was Arthur Tappan (1786–1865), who was born in Massachusetts and made a fortune in the dry goods business in New York City. His brother Lewis (1788–1873) joined him in the business and in 1841 established the first agency in the country to rate commercial credit. The Tappans were active in several causes and were generous with money gifts. Arthur gave money to help found Oberlin College in 1833.

When the Society met in 1840, William Lloyd Garrison (1805–79), the fiery abolitionist leader from Boston, brought enough followers with him so that they were able to seize control of the organization, which they did not think was radical enough. The New York abolitionists, led by Lewis Tappan, then formed the American and Foreign Anti-Slavery Society. Garrison, although he called for abolition by moral persuasion only, and was against both physical violence and political action, was the most violent of all in language. Garrison began his abolitionist career by helping to edit a paper in Baltimore in 1829. In less than a year he was tried for libel for accusing a Massachusetts shipowner of engaging in the illegal slave trade. He was convicted and served a short jail term. Returning to Boston, Garrison published the first issue of the *Liberator*, a paper he continued for thirty-five years, in January, 1831. In it he declared:

I am in earnest—I will not equivocate—I will not excuse—I will not retreat a single inch—AND I WILL BE HEARD.

As time passed, Garrison became ever more uncompromising, attacking other abolitionists he considered too moderate. He called the Constitution "a covenant with death and an agreement with Hell," and advocated the secession of the northern states. Garrison's stridency made him many enemies, and feeling against him culminated in a riot on October 21, 1835, at a meeting of the Boston Female Anti-Slavery Society. A mob of well-dressed middle- and upper-class people became so threatening that the mayor of Boston jailed Garrison for his own protection.

Other capable and forceful men were also among the leaders of the abolitionist movement. Benjamin Lundy (1789–1839), born in New Jersey of a Quaker family, was one of the pioneers. He established a newspaper, the *Genius of Universal Emancipation*, in 1821 and edited it in various cities until 1835. Lundy traveled widely on behalf of abolition, chiefly in the hope of developing colonization projects. Lundy's approach was comparatively mild but even so he was assaulted and injured in Baltimore in 1828 by angry slave traders.

Elijah P. Lovejoy (1802–37) was the martyr of the antislavery cause. In 1836 he established in Alton, Illinois, a paper called the *Observer*, in which he advocated immediate abolition. Three times a mob destroyed his press. The fourth time, on November 7, 1837, Lovejoy was killed by a mob while defending his press. Gamaliel Bailey (1807–59) was another editor whose equipment was destroyed by mobs but he escaped with his life. Bailey became editor of the *Philanthropist* in Cincinnati in 1837. His office was attacked three times by proslavery mobs and once was entirely destroyed. After 1847 he edited the *National Era*, an abolitionist weekly published in Washington.

Cassius Marcellus Clay (1810–1903) was born into a wealthy Kentucky family but turned against slavery. He freed his slaves, worth $40,000, in 1844 and borrowed $10,000 so he could purchase and free thirteen of their relatives. The following year he established an abolitionist paper, the *True American*, in Lexington, Kentucky. It was hardly under way when a mob, in his absence, raided the paper's office, dismantled all the equipment and shipped it off to Cincinnati. Clay had his press put back together and issued the paper from the northern side of the Ohio River. An outstanding orator in the cause of antislavery was Wendell Phillips (1811–84). An upper-class Bostonian, Phillips's career in the movement began with his eloquent and impassioned address in 1837 protesting the murder of Lovejoy.

Besides journalism and oratory, which for the most part reached only northerners, workers in the antislavery movement used pam-

phlets, posters, songs, fiction and poetry to find audiences in both the
North and the South. When it was learned in July, 1835, that
abolitionist propaganda from the North was arriving in the United
States mail at Charleston, a mob of local people raided the post office
and destroyed the offending material. Pictures were widely used to
reach the slaves. Songs, such as the collection *The Liberty Minstrel*, were
popular, as were groups like the singing Hutchinson Family of New
Hampshire who musically supported a number of reforms. Sheets
bearing antislavery statements quoted from the Bible, statesmen and
philosophers were circulated. Seals, similar to postage stamps, were
put on envelopes.

Activists were the victims of mob violence, in the North as well as
the South. Amos Dresser, a college student, was seized while selling
Bibles in Nashville, Tennessee, in 1835 and, an abolition newspaper
being found in his baggage, he was sentenced to twenty lashes and told
to leave town. The next year another theological student, Aaron W.
Kitchell, was taken by a mob in Hillsborough, Georgia, because he
was suspected of talking with slaves. He was whipped, tarred and
feathered. In the North, Marius Robinson was kidnaped after
lecturing in Berlin, Ohio, tarred and feathered and dumped by the
roadside. In New York City in July, 1834, a mob of proslavery
adherents went around the city attacking blacks and whites alike. The
home of Lewis Tappan was plundered, his furniture taken out to the
lawn and burned. Two white and three Negro churches were
damaged and the homes of twenty blacks destroyed.

The antislavery forces entered politics in 1840 with the formation
of the Liberty party. In the presidential election that year, the party
received only 7,059 votes but four years later, when the issue of the
admission of Texas to the Union aroused northerners, the party polled
62,300 votes. The party disappeared in 1848 when it merged with
other antislavery supporters to form the Free Soil party. The leader of
the Liberty party and its candidate for the presidency in 1840 and
1844 was James G. Birney (1792–1857) of Kentucky. Birney first

worked for the American Colonization Society but by 1834 he decided this scheme would not succeed. He became an abolitionist and freed the slaves he had inherited.

The quiet man of the abolitionist movement was Theodore D. Weld (1803–95), who as a young man became a disciple of the evangelist Charles G. Finney. A large, energetic man, Weld aided the Society for Promoting Manual Labor in Literary Institutions because he believed it was good for students to do their own chores. As early as 1830 he was a leader in the abolition movement and a founder of the American Anti-Slavery Society. In 1833, he led a number of theological students to Cincinnati to enter the newly founded Lane Seminary. The students became active in promoting the antislavery issue and were commanded by the trustees to stop. They refused and fifty-one of them went to Oberlin, Ohio, to enter the new college there. Weld was the author of *American Slavery as It Is* (1839), on which Harriet Beecher Stowe based her novel, *Uncle Tom's Cabin.*

One of the loneliest antislavery battles was fought almost single-handedly by former President John Quincy Adams. Two years after his term expired in 1829, Adams was elected to the House of Representatives, the only former president ever to serve there. About this time, abolitionists, spurred by the American Anti-Slavery Society, regularly flooded Congress with petitions, demanding the end of slavery in the District of Columbia. Southern representatives, with the aid of northern Democrats, passed a gag rule in 1834 which prevented such petitions from even being discussed in the House. While Adams did not like slavery, he was not an abolitionist, but he took up the cause of the right of the people to petition their government. Each year this aging New England gentleman fought the adoption of the gag rule. In 1842 it was approved by only four votes, in 1843 by only three votes, and the next year the House voted down the gag rule, 108 to 80. "Old Man Eloquent," as Adams had become known for his tenacious and logical arguments, was the victor at the age of seventy-seven. Adams continued to serve until 1848 when he collapsed on the floor of the House and died two days later.

Women were active in the abolition movement. They made significant contributions, particularly considering that they labored under the handicap of being thought, by some men, "unladylike" in getting involved in public affairs. Most of the women active in the antislavery movement were also advocates of women's rights and other reforms. When the American Anti-Slavery Society was formed, one woman spoke at the organization meeting, but none was asked to sign the founding declaration, or allowed to become a member. Membership was not opened to women until 1839. Women were encouraged to form their own groups and the first such convention was held in New York in May, 1837. Three hundred women from ten states attended. When a second assembly was held in Philadelphia in May, 1838, a mob burned the building. A World Anti-Slavery Convention was held in London in 1840, but women were refused admittance as full-fledged delegates.

The Grimké sisters, Sarah (1792–1873) and Angelina (1805–79), were the first American women to speak publicly in favor of abolition and women's rights. Born into a distinguished, slave-owning family in Charleston, the sisters converted to Quakerism. Oppressed by the proslavery atmosphere of their home state, they moved to Philadelphia in 1832 and soon became abolitionists. They sparked controversy in the northeast by lecturing widely. One New England clergyman said that "he would as soon be caught robbing a hen roost as encouraging a woman to lecture." Sarah contended that "whatsoever it is morally right for a man to do, it is morally right for a woman to do." Angelina married Theodore Weld in 1838. A year earlier she wrote him after a lecture: "I cannot help smiling . . . to witness their perfect amazement at hearing a woman speak in the churches."

Many free blacks took part in the movement to liberate the slaves, and some served as agents of the American Anti-Slavery

Society. Among the blacks involved were David Walker (1785–1830), Sojourner Truth (c.1797–1833) and Frederick Douglass (1817–95). Walker, the son of a free mother and a slave father, was born in North Carolina. He moved north and became an antislavery activist in Boston. His chief contribution was an 1829 pamphlet entitled *An Appeal to the Coloured Citizens of the World*. It was an eloquent description of actual slave conditions, and urged the blacks to revolt. Sojourner Truth was born a slave in New York but became free when that state abolished slavery. Believing heavenly voices told her to aid her people, she traveled through the North speaking for abolition and women's rights. Although illiterate, she was an effective lecturer and captured her audiences with her personality.

Douglass was the outstanding black abolitionist. Born in Maryland, the son of a slave and a white man, Douglass escaped to the North in 1838. Three years later he made his first antislavery speech. Tall, with flashing eyes and a melodious voice, Douglass was soon an unusually effective orator. His autobiography, *Narrative of the Life of Frederick Douglass*, appeared in 1845 and in it, writing of the terrible decision as to whether to try to escape, he recalled:

> In coming to a fixed determination to run away, we did more than Patrick Henry, when he resolved upon liberty or death. With us it was a doubtful liberty at most, and almost certain death if we failed. For my part, I should prefer death to hopeless bondage.

Douglass went to Great Britain and Ireland that year and remained away for two years, fearful that he might be seized and returned to slavery. With his freedom purchased by English friends, he returned and established an abolitionist paper, the *North Star*, in Rochester, New York, which he edited until 1864. Douglass believed in a political approach to the slavery problem and was a follower of James G. Birney.

The most dramatic of the abolitionists' activities was the "Underground Railroad." Helping slaves escape to freedom was not new, but in the second quarter of the century it became a more organized operation. Stimulated by the coming of the railroad age, abolitionists used terms such as station for a place where slaves were collected, and conductor for a person who led slaves to freedom. "Underground Railroad" seems to have been first used in 1831. The system assisted thousands of slaves to escape to the North or to Canada, and more than 3,000 persons were active in its work. Various methods and all kinds of tricks were used to aid the slaves—at least one black, Henry "Box" Brown, escaped from Richmond to Philadelphia by being shipped express in a box.

Because of his work for the Underground Railroad, Levi Coffin (1798–1877) was known as its "president." Born in North Carolina, he moved to Fountain City, Indiana, where his home was a leading station. He is said to have assisted 3,000 slaves. Harriet Tubman (c.1820–1913), an illiterate field hand who escaped from slavery in Maryland in 1849, became an expert at guiding escapees. She helped more than 300, and if timid ones lagged after the march started, she held a pistol on them. The Reverend John Rankin, who left Tennessee to live in Ripley, Ohio, overlooking the river, set up the best-known station on the railroad. The real Eliza, made famous in *Uncle Tom's Cabin*, crossed the ice of the Ohio River here in the early 1830's. John Fairfield, son of a slaveholding Virginia family, was one of the most daring and ingenious workers. He posed as a slave trader and in other guises in leading slaves northward. One time he escaped with twenty-eight slaves by organizing a false funeral procession.

Despite their efforts, the abolitionists did not seem to be making much progress by 1850. Only a small proportion of the inhabitants of the northern states showed active interest and there was some opposition. The protests against the Mexican War and the annexation of Texas indicated some growth in antislavery sentiment, but the abolitionists' words and deeds hardened the southern proslavery stand.

14 An Age of Reform

FROM ABOUT 1825 until the outbreak of the Civil War in 1861, the atmosphere in the nation was one of reform. Although most noticeable because most controversial, the antislavery movement was but one of many causes for which people organized, labored and contributed money. Dedicated people worked for women's rights, prison reform, educational reform, religious liberalism, social welfare and other causes. As one clergyman summed up, there were

> missionary societies, tract societies, education societies, moral societies, and other societies of various names for the purposes of feeding the hungry, clothing the naked, instructing the ignorant, saving the lost, and promoting peace on earth and mutual amity among mankind.

And there was even a group called the Society to Improve the Condition of the Sailors. The core of the reform movement consisted of middle-class, Protestant Americans, and was centered, geographically, in New England.

Many causes lay behind this outpouring of a desire to do good. Most immediate was the religious revival that began in the 1820's. In addition, the rational spirit of the eighteenth-century Enlightenment, with its idea of the possibility of progress if people consciously worked toward that end, remained influential. The newer spirit of Romanticism, which advocated a return to nature and a belief in the essential goodness of humanity, was related to the older notion that the New

World was a second Eden where people could start over. To all this was added the democratic spirit of equality and the goal of Utilitarianism: the achievement of the greatest happiness for the greatest number.

Utopianism—the establishment of an ideal society—was the most exotic of the reform movements. Behind utopianism were socialist political and economic theory and religious eccentricity, sometimes mingled. Socialist utopianism in America took its theory largely from Charles Fourier (1772–1837), a French social philosopher who worked out a scheme of organizing human beings into economic units called phalanxes. Each phalanx was to consist of 1,620 people who would live in a phalanstery, a community building. The members would work according to their natural inclinations, and Fourier's society was basically an agricultural one.

His ideas were tried in the United States by Albert Brisbane (1809–90), the son of a wealthy landowner. On a trip to Europe, Brisbane met Fourier and studied under him. Returning home, Brisbane set out to organize phalanxes, except that he used the term Associationism for his version of the system. By interesting Horace Greeley, the editor of the New York *Tribune*, in his schemes, Brisbane secured a great deal of publicity. He also wrote a book, *The Social Destiny of Man* (1840). In it he declared the family was an outworn institution, children should be so trained that they became productive members of society by the age of three and women should not be confined to the home. Brisbane helped start over forty socialized communities, most of which soon failed.

Best known of these communities, and the longest lasting, was the North American Phalanx at Red Bank, New Jersey. It was founded in 1843 and survived until 1854. A total of 1,200 persons formed the group, which had a large area of fertile land and a three-story phalanstery. It was an agrarian and handicraft economy which owed its success to its truck garden products that had a good market in nearby urban centers.

Étienne Cabet (1788–1856) was another French utopian philosopher whose theories were tried in America. His book, *Voyage en Icarie* (1840), described a community in which an elected council ruled all economic and social activity, leaving the family as the only other independent unit. About 500 followers set up an Icarian community on the Red River in Texas in 1848, but it failed. The next year Cabet founded a unit in the old Mormon town of Nauvoo, Illinois, but dissension arose and in 1856 the colonists refused to reelect him president.

The most intellectual of all utopian settlements was Brook Farm—actually the Brook Farm Association for Industry and Education—near Boston, established in 1841. Brook Farm's leader and founder, along with his wife, Sophia, was George Ripley (1802–80), a literary critic and one of the group of New England literary and intellectual leaders known as the Transcendentalists. Brook Farm was based on "plain living and high thinking." The 192-acre farm was to be worked cooperatively by all the members. This would provide food and make them self-sufficient so they could spend much of their time thinking, talking and writing. They were not experienced farmers and did not do well economically. In 1844 Brisbane convinced the members they should become a phalanx. They agreed but in 1846 the unfinished phalanstery building burned down, uninsured, and the Brook Farm experiment ended.

The novelist Nathaniel Hawthorne was a member of Brook Farm for a short time and used the experience in his novel *The Blithedale Romance* (1852). In it the narrator remarks:

> Persons of marked individuality—crooked sticks, as some of us might be called—are not exactly the easiest to bind into a fagot . . . . Our labor symbolized nothing, and left us mentally sluggish in the dusk of the evening. Intellectual activity is incompatible with any large amount of bodily exercise.

Another utopian experiment in New England was even more

short-lived. This was Fruitlands, sponsored by Bronson Alcott (1799–1888), whose contributions to educational theory and practice were substantial. Alcott was a peddler and worked in a clock factory before becoming a teacher. He founded the Temple School at Boston and conducted it from 1834 to 1839. He sought to develop the whole person in harmonious surroundings, advocated a conversational method of instruction, and introduced organized play and the honor system. His ideas were too advanced and he closed the school. He later became superintendent of the Concord, Massachusetts, schools and put into the curriculum for the first time subjects such as physiology, dancing and reading aloud. Alcott's Fruitlands was established on a small farm near Cambridge in 1843, and lasted about seven months. His family and a small group of friends tried a communal and vegetarian existence which didn't prove practical.

A number of organizations sought utopia in communities based on religious beliefs. Among such groups were the Mormons, the Shakers, the Oneida Community and the Amana Society. Of them all, the Mormons were the most successful. The history of the Mormons, the name commonly given to members of the Church of Jesus Christ of Latter-Day Saints, began in Palmyra, New York, in 1827 when young Joseph Smith (1805–44) reported he had unearthed some golden tablets, the writing on which he translated and published in 1829 as the *Book of Mormon*. The revelation of these tablets and other visions led him to found his church in 1830. He quickly attracted a number of followers and in 1831 set up the church's headquarters in Kirtland, Ohio. The *Book of Mormon* reputed to be the account by the prophet Mormon of the early history of one of the lost tribes of Israel in America. Mormon also revealed God's special message for America. This made a distinctively American religion of Mormonism at a time when nationalistic feeling was strong.

The Mormons moved on to Independence, Missouri, but met with hostility—partly because of their beliefs, and partly because their close-knit, communal economic organization gave them a high degree of efficiency. Ordered out of the state, they moved back east to Nauvoo, Illinois. By 1844 Nauvoo was the largest and most prosperous city in Illinois, with a population of about 15,000. Again the Mormons were distrusted for their beliefs and disliked for their economic competition. Feeling against them turned dangerous after Smith proclaimed the doctrine of polygamy as part of the Mormon order in 1843. Smith and his brother were arrested in June, 1844, when there was an uprising against the Mormons. A mob broke into the jail and lynched Smith and his brother.

Leadership of the Mormons fell into the strong hands of Brigham Young (1801–77) who, like Smith, was born in Vermont. He had been a carpenter and glazier in western New York when he joined the new church. In 1846 Young began to organize a migration from Illinois all the way to the area of the Great Salt Lake, in Utah. The Mormons moved west in small groups, using specially constructed carts that could be hauled by men. The first Mormons reached their goal in July, 1847, and by fall 1,800 had arrived. A similar number reached the land the Mormons called Deseret the following year. Salt Lake City was laid out, families were assigned lots and farms, an efficient irrigation system was built and water was allotted each farmer. When Congress in 1850 created Utah Territory, covering roughly the area of the present states of Utah and Nevada, Young was appointed governor and ruled over the region benevolently and theocratically.

Less aggressive in religion and economics than the Mormons was the United Society of Believers in Christ's Second Appearing, better known as the Shakers, and so-called because their fervent religious emotion at times caused them to tremble and shake. The Shakers developed out of a religious revival among Quakers in England in 1747, and they established themselves in America in 1774 when "Mother" Ann Lee (1736–84) brought a group of eight followers to New York. An illiterate mystic, Mother Ann taught belief in the dual nature of the deity, the male principle being exhibited in Jesus Christ, the female in her. After her death the movement prospered and communal groups spread as far west as Indiana by 1826. The Shakers believed in celibacy, possession of goods in common, equality of the sexes and pacifism. Their life was simple and strictly controlled. For social conversation, two rows of chairs were arranged facing each other, the men sitting in one row, the women in the other. Of all the utopian groups, the Shakers were the only ones to develop a distinctive architectural style. Buildings and furniture were functional, plain and with clean lines, considerably different from the popular taste of the day. The Shakers were excellent farmers and craftsmen, and their products were highly regarded.

Like the Shakers, the Perfectionists followed the lead of a prophet and were successful in their economic life. Perfectionism taught that people could become perfect here on earth if they freed themselves from selfishness. As a group, the Perfectionists held all property in common, operated a complex marriage system and provided communal care for the children. The founder and leader of the Perfectionists was John Humphrey Noyes (1811–86), born in Vermont, where in 1839 he set up his first community. The marriage system he introduced, which was a form of polygamy, outraged his neighbors and the colony was forced to flee. Noyes led a migration to New York State where the group established the Oneida Community. People of more orthodox opinion threatened them here also, but the community was prosperous as a result of the steel traps and silverware it produced.

The Amana Society originated as a Pietist religious sect in eighteenth-century Germany. Under the leadership of Christian Metz (1794–1867), about 600 persons came to the United States and settled near Buffalo, New York, in 1843. They were a well-to-do and highly organized body whose communal way of life worked. They acquired 20,000 acres of land in Iowa to which they moved in 1855, and they established a successful cooperative industry.

Only the abolitionist crusade created more controversy than the women's rights movement. Fundamentally, the cause of women's rights was based on the tenets of American democracy. If all men were equal, then all women should be equal also. Females, as they were usually referred to, should have the same social, legal, political and economic rights as their fathers, husbands and sons. When women leaders found they were barred from, or at least unwelcome in, the early antislavery movement, they decided they had to establish their general rights in order to gain roles in other reform activities.

Spurred by such events as their rebuff at the London antislavery conference, a group of women called a convention to be held in Seneca Falls, New York, in July, 1848. There the women formulated a "Declaration of Sentiments," which cleverly paraphrased the Declaration of Independence, substituting "man" for King George III. The document called for women's "immediate admission to all the rights and privileges which belong to them as citizens of the United States." The women also noted solemnly that "in entering upon the great work before us, we anticipate no small amount of misconception, misrepresentation, and ridicule."

Lucretia Mott (1793–1880) and Elizabeth Cady Stanton (1815–1902) were the organizers of the Seneca Falls Convention, and with Susan B. Anthony (1820–1906) provided leadership for the women's movement for many years. Mrs. Mott, a Quaker by birth, was one of the earliest women lecturers for temperance, world peace, the rights of labor, and abolition. In 1811 she married James Mott (1788–1868), who worked for abolition and woman suffrage and, at the request of the organizers, presided at the Seneca Falls Convention. Mrs. Mott's home in Philadelphia was a station on the Underground Railroad. Mrs. Stanton was particularly interested in securing the right to vote and insisted that such a clause be included in the declaration at Seneca Falls. When she married Henry B. Stanton in 1840, she refused to have the word "obey" used in the ceremony. Mrs. Stanton was an effective orator and writer. Miss Anthony, a schoolteacher at seventeen, agitated for equal pay for women teachers and for coeducation and college training for girls. When the Sons of Temperance refused to admit women, she founded a women's temperance organization.

Lucy Stone (1818–93) and Amelia Bloomer (1818–94) were ridiculed by some for their actions. Miss Stone, who graduated from Oberlin College in 1847 and the same year began to lecture on women's rights, insisted on keeping her own name when she married Henry Brown Blackwell (1825–1909). Blackwell was also a reformer. Miss Bloomer edited the *Lily*, a women's rights and temperance magazine, from 1848 to 1854. In 1851 she began wearing a skirt over full trousers, much like Turkish trousers. She advocated the costume in print and wore it when she lectured. As a result, it became known by her name, although it was designed in the 1840's by Mrs. Elizabeth Smith Miller.

Important contributions were made by Elizabeth Peabody (1804–94) and Margaret Fuller (1810–50). Miss Peabody was a member of the Massachusetts intellectual group whose special interest was educational reform. She was also an abolitionist and for a while she ran a bookstore from her home. Miss Peabody assisted Bronson Alcott in his Temple School and later wrote an account of his theories. She opened the first kindergarten in an English-speaking country in 1860. Miss Fuller was one of the liveliest literary personalities of the day and took an active part in the intellectual life of the Transcendentalists. She was educated by her father who made her study Latin at the age of six. Her conversation classes on literary and social subjects, which she conducted in Boston from 1839 to 1844, were stimulating events for the women who attended. Out of her experience she wrote *Woman in the Nineteenth Century* (1844), the first important study of feminism in America, and a daring book for its time. She wrote frankly about sexual as well as political, economic and intellectual aspects of feminism. From 1840 to 1841 she edited the *Dial*, the journal of the Boston intellectuals.

The struggle for women's rights bore a few early fruits. Mississippi in 1839 gave women the right to hold property, while New York, Indiana and Pennsylvania followed in 1849, and California and Wisconsin in 1850. The New York law, however, was of benefit primarily to the well-to-do. It gave a wife control of her property at the time of marriage and excepted it from any attachment for her husband's debts, but wages earned by a wife still belonged to the husband.

After abolition and women's rights, no reform movement attracted as much attention as the temperance crusade. That drinking was widespread and often carried to excess was attested to by every commentator. The crusade, which began by stressing temperance but turned into a drive for complete abstention, was conducted as a moral movement and its leadership came primarily from the Protestant clergy. Many employers felt their workers would be more efficient if they did not drink. The American Temperance Society was organized in 1826, and under the name American Temperance Union held its first national convention ten years later. The movement spread, and in 1834 the North Carolina Temperance Society, for example, claimed fifty branches with 4,700 members. The Washingtonian Movement of 1840 gathered together reformed drinkers, much like the modern Alcoholics Anonymous. The Order of the Sons of Temperance was formed at Teetotaler's Hall in New York in 1842, and by 1850 had 200,000 members. A temperance novel, *My Mother's Gold Ring*, by Lucius Manlius Sargent was published in 1833 and sold 113,000 copies. Maine was the first state to pass a prohibition law, in 1846, and by 1855 fourteen states and territories had followed.

Neal Dow (1804–97), born in Maine of a Quaker family, was largely responsible for prohibition in that state and drafted a revised and more rigid law in 1851. Dow, who made his first temperance speech when he was twenty-four, was also strongly abolitionist. The most sensational of the temperance lecturers was John Bartholomew Gough (1817–86), an Englishman who was a former alcoholic. Beginning in 1845 he lectured for forty years and thousands signed the teetotaler's pledge after hearing his horrendous story of the evils of drink.

Agitation for the reform of prisons, poorhouses and asylums was another significant movement of the time. Foremost in effort and effectiveness was Dorothea Dix (1802–87), who began her career as a teacher. An 1841 visit to a jail in East Cambridge, Massachusetts, shocked her with its deplorable conditions, including the mixing of criminals and the insane. She prepared a report to the state legislature in January, 1843, after inspecting other jails. She described the insane as "chained, naked, beaten with rods and lashed into obedience." Between her first visit and 1844, she inspected 18 state penitentiaries, 300 county jails and houses of correction, and more than 500 poorhouses and similar institutions. Her work resulted in the establishment of publicly supported hospitals for the mentally ill in fifteen states.

The campaign for world peace made little progress, although some of the opposition to the Mexican War came out of general anti-war attitudes. America's most effective worker for peace was Elihu Burritt (1810–79), sometimes called "the learned blacksmith." While an apprentice, he taught himself many subjects, especially languages of which it was said he could read fifty. Interested in many reforms, he edited the *Christian Citizen* from 1844 to 1851. Burritt organized the League of Human Brotherhood in 1846 with some English pacifists.

Failure to achieve their goals quickly did not discourage the reformers, and the same spirit prevailed in religion and education, which were also subject to the reforming mood of the times.

15   Religion and Education

"THERE IS no country in the world," the French commentator Tocqueville decided, "in which the Christian religion retains a greater influence over the souls of men than in America." But he added that "in the United States religion exercises but little influence upon the laws." Even though life was more secularized than in earlier times, more Americans were church members than ever before. After the wave of revivalism that swept parts of the countryside in the 1820's and 1830's, another in the 1840's produced many converts in the cities. Whereas in 1800 about one out of fifteen Americans was a church member, by 1850 it was estimated that one out of seven had some religious affiliation.

The series of revivals resulted by 1850 in the domination of Protestant religious life by the Methodists and the Baptists. They numbered well over half of all Protestants. These two groups grew from small sects to major denominations because they rebelled against the Calvinistic doctrine that every person was predestined to be saved or not. They believed that by living a life free of sin and by doing good, a person could earn a place among the chosen. Many blacks, attracted to the Methodist and Baptist faiths, organized their own churches. At least 6,000 blacks were church members in Charleston in 1845, and before that Louisville had four black churches—three Methodist and one Baptist.

The controversy over slavery, however, disrupted the two leading denominations. A movement began in the early 1830's within the Methodists to bring the church to an antislavery stand, and when a General Conference was held in 1844, they moved a small step toward abolitionism by deposing a bishop who was a slaveholder. At another meeting in Louisville in 1845, the southern Methodists seceded and established the Methodist Episcopal Church, South. The Baptists, with a looser form of organization, also disagreed among themselves and antislavery and proslavery groups formed. The Southern Baptist Convention met in 1845, and a northern group held a separate meeting.

No religious group grew nearly as fast as the Roman Catholics. With only 600,000 American Catholics in 1830, their numbers increased to 3,500,000 in 1850. This increase was caused chiefly by heavy immigration from Ireland. Immigration from Germany also brought in some Catholics. Most of the Germans, however, and almost all the Scandinavians—who were beginning to emigrate in large numbers to take up farms on the frontier—were Lutherans. By 1850, the Catholics were the largest single denomination, followed by the Methodists and the Baptists. The once-large Presbyterian and Congregational denominations ranked fourth and fifth, the Lutherans were sixth and the Disciples of Christ seventh. The Episcopalians, the most important denomination at the time of the Revolution, were eighth in size.

A new group of small denominations, called Adventists, grew from the beliefs and teachings of William Miller (1782–1849). In 1831 Miller predicted that on March 21, 1843, at three A.M., the present world would come to an end with the return of Christ, who would raise the dead, gather up his saints and usher in the millennium. Miller's followers grew to about 1,000,000, and some prepared special ascension robes. Even though the second coming of Christ did not occur, Adventists continued to believe that it would. The largest Adventist body in 1844 adopted Saturday as the Sabbath and became the Seventh-Day Adventists.

A number of unusual people, some conservative, some liberal, and some who found it difficult to decide just where they stood in the matter of religion, left their mark on the period. One such man was Peter Cartwright (1785–1872), a Methodist minister who preached salvation for nearly fifty years as a "circuit rider," a preacher who traveled a large area on horseback, holding religious meetings wherever he went. Cartwright once preached for several days in Waynesville, Illinois, which he called "a very wicked little village." After a man who tried to break up one of his meetings was accidentally killed the same day, Cartwright noted that "the whole country was in an agony for salvation." Charles G. Finney could also affect a congregation. "The Lord let me loose upon them in a wonderful manner," he wrote of one occasion when he had almost the whole congregation on their knees.

Horace Bushnell (1802–76), a Congregational minister in Connecticut, was the intellectual leader of liberal Christianity. He emphasized the divine in humanity and nature, and refused to accept the harsh Calvinistic view of humanity. Although accused of heresy for his views on the Trinity, he was not tried.

Americans put a great deal of faith in education, as well as in religion. A strong feeling existed that in a democracy where suffrage was widespread, an educated people was a necessity if the democracy was to succeed. Schools could also help unify so large a nation and breed a spirit of national feeling. Furthermore, as the number of immigrants increased, many persons felt that the only hope of "Americanizing" the children of these strangers was through the school system. By 1850, in the North and the West, the principle was established that all children were entitled to a primary school education in tax-supported and government-supervised schools. The extension of the same principle to the secondary school level began in the 1830's, but was not everywhere accepted by 1850.

The progress of public education varied from state to state. It was estimated that in 1833, 1,000,000 young Americans between the ages of five and fifteen were not attending school. The following year Pennsylvania enacted a public education law, but a few years later half the children in that state were not in school. New York State passed a public school education bill in 1849, but both here and in Pennsylvania, localities had the option of deciding not to support schools free to everyone. Grants of public land, the income from which was used for education, helped speed the coming of public schools in the Old Northwest. The South lagged in public school education. In 1850 in the South Central States only one white child in ten was in school, while in the North Central States, one of five went to school. White illiteracy in the South was five times that of New England.

The South, however, had a better record in the matter of academies. These schools, some privately owned, some sponsored by religious denominations, offered education that sometimes went beyond high school subjects. In many places, and while the public school system at the secondary level was in its infancy, these academies offered the best educational facilities. There were 6,000 or more academies in 1850, and the South accounted for 2,700.

Another principle established by mid-century was that teachers should be professionally educated. New York State in 1829 became one of the first states to require some proof of character ("unimpeachable") and "the requisite literary qualification." That year a committee in Philadelphia found that many of the city's teachers were "destitute of all moral character, often grossly ignorant." It was not until 1839 that any state, in this case Massachusetts, established a state-supported school to train teachers.

The founding of that school was one of the many accomplishments of Horace Mann (1796–1859), who contributed more than any other person to educational reform. Giving up a lucrative law practice and a high position in the Massachusetts legislature, Mann became secretary of the board of education of the state in 1837. He served about a dozen years and transformed the Massachusetts school system, and also influenced public school education all over the country.

Mann instituted longer school terms, demanded better schoolhouses, and secured higher pay for teachers. Fifty new high schools were built while he served. Mann insisted on non-sectarian education, which caused some of the clergy to attack him.

In the neighboring state of Connecticut, Henry Barnard (1811–1900) followed much the same path as Mann. He helped enact legislation in 1838 to improve state supervision of Connecticut's schools and then took on the job of administering the law. He instituted better school inspection, more systematic selection of textbooks, and sponsored joint meetings of parents and teachers. Barnard surveyed the Rhode Island school system in 1843 and one of his recommendations resulted in the setting up of school libraries.

Calvin E. Stowe (1802–86), after teaching Greek at Dartmouth College, moved to Cincinnati, Ohio, in 1833 to teach Biblical literature at Lane Seminary. Three years later he married Harriet Beecher, daughter of the president of the seminary, Lyman Beecher, and later the author of *Uncle Tom's Cabin*. Stowe was appointed a member of a commission to study European schools and his 1837 report provided the basis for the public school system of Ohio. It called for state control over local school boards, a principle adopted later in other states.

The increase in the number of colleges, from 173 to 239 in the decade of the 1840's, was impressive but not as substantial as it sounded. Most of the increase was accounted for by small denominational institutions as part of the evangelical effort in the West. They were mostly poorly staffed, under-financed and offered a small number of courses, some of which were not at the college level. Many were short-lived. At this time only about 2 per cent of the college-age population attended college. The state-supported university systems were just starting. Michigan pioneered with a law creating a state university in 1847, but gave it little support for some time.

As the democratic ideal spread in American life, agitation began for more "practical" training in college. The Massachusetts legislature criticized Harvard for not training its students to become "better farmers, mechanics or merchants." Francis Wayland (1796–1865) was one educator who caused some changes in higher education. After serving as a clergyman in Boston, he became president of Brown University in 1827 and remained there until 1855. Wayland instituted flexible entrance requirements and the offering of elective courses. He wanted student bodies to be more widely representative of the total population and proposed to offer courses in economics, applied science, agriculture and teaching methods. One of his reports proposed that "every student might study what he chose, all that he chose, and nothing but what he chose."

The increase in the number of colleges did little to make higher education available to women. Oberlin was the first coeducational college and had forty students in its Female Department in 1834. Three years later four young women entered Oberlin at the college level and became candidates for a degree which three received in 1841. Mount Holyoke College, in South Hadley, Massachusetts, the first permanent women's college, was founded by Mary Lyon (1797–1849) in 1837. Miss Lyon, a teacher, was principal for twelve years. Catherine Beecher (1800–78), another daughter of Lyman, founded a girls' school in Hartford, Connecticut, in 1824 and later went west where she established several seminaries for women. She introduced domestic science into her schools. Although she was a strong advocate of education for women, she opposed woman suffrage. In a report in 1829 she wrote:

> If all females were not only well educated themselves, but were prepared to communicate in an easy manner their stores of knowledge to others, if they not only knew how to regulate their own minds, tempers and habits, but how to effect improvements in those around them, the face of society would speedily be changed.

Practical and effective work with the handicapped was undertaken, particularly by Samuel Gridley Howe (1801–76) who received a medical degree from Harvard in 1824. He spent the next six years in Greece which was then fighting Turkey for independence. He gave medical assistance, distributed food and clothing and aided in rebuilding after freedom was won. Back in the United States, Howe established the New England Asylum for the Blind (later the Perkins Institution) in 1831 and remained its head for nearly forty-five years. Howe's star pupil was Laura Bridgman (1829–89) who as a result of an illness at the age of two lost all her senses, except that of touch. When she was eight, Howe took her into his school where she learned to read and write and to sew. She remained at the school to teach sewing. Laura was the first blind and deaf person to be educated successfully.

While a better educational system was developing, especially in the North and West, blacks were mostly restricted to separate schools, even in free territory. A judicial decision in 1849 laid down a rule that was not changed for over a hundred years. Lemuel Shaw, chief justice of the highest Massachusetts court, decided in *Roberts* v. *City of Boston* that separate but equal school facilities were legal. The question arose in the matter of requiring a black child to attend a school for Negroes. However, blacks made some progress in securing admission to higher educational facilities. Along with Oberlin, Dartmouth and Western Reserve admitted black students.

Horace Mann had lasting influence on educational systems, but two other people had more to do with what thousands of students actually learned in American schools: Noah Webster (1758–1843) and William Holmes McGuffey (1800–73). Webster's most valuable work was the *American Dictionary of the English Language*, issued in 1828 and revised in 1840. It defined 12,000 words not in any other dictionary, its definitions were good, it helped standardize pronunciation in America and it reached a sale of 300,000 a year. Webster's most influential work was his *Elementary Spelling Book*, the first edition of which appeared before the turn of the century. It was used in almost every school in the country. By 1837 it had sold 15,000,000 copies and in

1850 it was selling at the unheard of rate of 1,000,000 copies a year. The speller spread the spirit of nationalism by distinguishing between American and British spelling and pronunciation.

McGuffey's *Eclectic Readers* did even more to shape the minds and attitudes of young Americans. A college teacher and president, McGuffey issued six readers between 1836 and 1857. Thus the main textbook for students the country over for their first six years of schooling was a McGuffey product. It is estimated that around 122,000,000 copies were sold. Reading the selections, a student was taught morality, patriotism and faith in progress. The selections came from American and British writers of the best quality: Shakespeare, Dr. Johnson, Daniel Webster, Longfellow and many others. McGuffey also included less substantial but possibly more interesting material: a biography of Napoleon Bonaparte and a piece that explained "How a Fly Walks on the Ceiling." He included a piece on the law concerning private property and an essay entitled "God Blesses the Industrious." The nationwide use of these books not only set cultural patterns, but also spread a common body of knowledge throughout the country.

Adult education flourished through the "lyceum," a voluntary association for disseminating information and opinion. The first lyceum was established in Millbury, Massachusetts, in 1826 by Josiah Holbrook (1788–1854). Holbrook was a teacher whose Agricultural Seminary failed in 1825. He was interested in natural science and organized these community groups to popularize his favorite subject. Within two years he helped establish more than a hundred lyceums. The National American Lyceum was formed in 1831 and by 1834, 3,000 lyceums existed. They were mostly in the North, although the spread westward was rapid and reached as far as Iowa and Minnesota. The subject matter of the forums and lectures increased to cover just about everything, including contemporary affairs. The lyceum movement provided excellent platforms for reformers. The best-known statesmen and writers of the day, such as Daniel Webster and Ralph Waldo Emerson, appeared on lyceum platforms.

The quarter century ending in 1850 was a significant one in the fields of religion and education. Many changes took place, and in education the groundwork was laid for a complete system of free education.

THE FERMENT of the period in politics, reform, religion and education was matched in the intellectual and literary world. Ralph Waldo Emerson remarked in 1844 that everyone should be struck by the "great activity of thought and experimenting." He was referring to New England, and while most of the intellectual ferment took place in the northeast, the whole nation was affected.

Three words—Transcendentalism, Romanticism and nationalism—sum up the world of ideas that concerned the thinkers and writers of the time. Transcendentalism was the intellectual product of a small group of unusually intelligent men and women, and was centered in Concord, Massachusetts. Like Unitarianism, with which it had much in common, Transcendentalism was a reaction against the cold rationalism of the eighteenth-century Enlightenment and the grim Calvinism of New England orthodoxy. More a way of thinking than a systematic philosophy, Transcendentalism had a mystical cast. The individual and his or her intuition were emphasized, and the establishment of a direct relationship with nature, where harmony can be found, was stressed. The divinity of God, said the Transcendentalists, dwells in everything in the world. The soul, therefore, can contain all that the world contains and people can discover truth through their own insights. Transcendentalism glorified the individual, who was to be optimistic and self-reliant. As Emerson said: "Let man stand erect, go alone and possess the universe." This contention that a person could rise to any height had great influence on the reformers.

Many elements from the past went into the making of Transcendentalism, but it also owed much to the newer Romantic movement, which began in Europe. Romanticism, too, put the individual in first place and it was sympathetic to the spirit of the United States, a country where the individual had to be self-reliant. The leader of the Transcendentalists and, indeed, the leader of the American intellectual and literary world for a generation or more, was Ralph Waldo Emerson (1803–82). Born in Boston and a descendant of a number of Puritan clergymen, Emerson trained for the ministry and in 1829 became pastor of the Old North Church (Unitarian) in Boston. Three years later, deciding his conscience would no longer let him administer the Lord's Supper, he resigned and traveled in Europe. Here, in his contacts with Continental and British men of letters, his interest in transcendental thought bloomed. He first set forth the principles of Transcendentalism in his essay *Nature* (1836), declaring his belief in the mystical unity of nature. The following year his Phi Beta Kappa address at Harvard, published as *The American Scholar*, was hailed as a declaration of intellectual independence, not just from Europe, but from anything that fettered thought.

> Our day of dependence, our long apprenticeship to the learning of other lands, draws to a close . . . . We have listened too long to the courtly muses of Europe . . . . We will walk on our own feet, we will work with our own hands; we will speak our own minds . . . . A nation of men will for the first time exist, because each believes himself inspired by the Divine Soul which also inspires all men.

Another address at Harvard, this time at the Divinity School in 1838, created a stir when he declared that only in one's own soul could redemption be found. Some listeners took this to be a repudiation of Christianity, and Emerson was not invited to speak at Harvard again until 1866. He continued keeping his journals, delivering lectures and writing his essays. One collection of *Essays* appeared in 1841, another in 1844. Emerson was also a poet, although not a great one, and a book of *Poems* was published in 1847. His other important work by mid-century was *Representative Men* (1850). Emerson was extremely popular as a public speaker and traveled widely every year, eventually as far as the Mississippi, to lecture from lyceum platforms. Emerson's influence on American life cannot be overestimated, although he played but little direct part himself in any reform movement or in politics. He took a large view:

> The power which is at once spring and regulator in all efforts of reform is the conviction that there is an infinite worthiness in man, which will appear at the call of worth, and that all particular reforms are the removing of some impediment.

Quite unlike Emerson, but still a thoroughgoing Transcendentalist was that unique American, Henry David Thoreau (1817–62). Thoreau tried teaching and surveying, and from 1841 to 1843 he lived in the Emerson household, where he acted as handyman and caretaker. From July, 1845, until September, 1847, he lived in a one-room hut he built at Walden Pond, near Concord, writing, thinking, observing nature and raising vegetables. During this period he was arrested for failing to pay his poll tax because he opposed the Mexican War. He was in jail only overnight because a friend paid his tax, much to his distress. As soon as he was released, he set off to pick some blueberries. An account of one of his experiences, *A Week on the Concord and Merrimack Rivers*, was published in 1849. So was *Civil Disobedience*, in which he wrote:

> Under a government which imprisons any unjustly, the true place for a just man is also in prison . . . . I, Henry Thoreau, do not wish to be regarded as a member of any incorporated society which I have not joined . . . .

Theodore Parker (1810–60) was another New England Transcendentalist whose beliefs as a clergyman were too liberal even for the Unitarians. He found a new preaching post in 1845 with the Twenty-Eighth Congregational Society of Boston where the membership grew to 7,000. From the pulpit and from the lyceum platform, Parker spoke for the abolitionist movement and other reforms.

Transcendentalist thought had a profound influence on many of the authors of the time, but a more tangible factor was nationalism. Almost everyone agreed that American literature should be American, should have American themes and reflect American democracy. Given a common language with England, a good deal of common history and the literary heritage of hundreds of writers, it was difficult to be completely American. That it was possible was shown in the work of the older generation, writers such as Washington Irving (1783–1859), James Fenimore Cooper (1789–1851) and James Kirke Paulding (1778–1860).

Irving treated some subjects not directly connected with America, but he never strayed far. His reputation was well established by 1825, and he enjoyed an international reputation for many years. His biography of Christopher Columbus appeared in 1828, *The Conquest of Granada*, about Spain and the Moors, in 1829, and *The Alhambra*, recounting Spanish legends, in 1832. Back in the United States after seventeen years in Europe, Irving went on a trip to the West, described in *A Tour of the Prairies* (1835). He also wrote, with the assistance of John Jacob Astor's records, an account of Astor's fur-trading business in *Astoria* (1836). *The Adventures of Captain Bonneville, U.S.A.* (1837) continued Irving's interest in the American West and helped make a hero out of its subject.

Cooper was a popular novelist before 1825 and in the ensuing years earned the right to be called America's first major novelist. The first of the Leather-Stocking Tales appeared in 1823 and the most popular of the five, *The Last of the Mohicans*, in 1826. Cooper wrote three more novels in which Natty Bumpo, the pioneer scout, was the hero: *The Prairie* (1827), *The Pathfinder* (1840) and *The Deerslayer* (1841).

All were successful and Cooper's main character was much admired as the perfect American frontiersman. Cooper romanticized the Indians, but his stories portrayed dramatically the clash between wilderness life and the civilization encroaching on it. Paulding in some of his early work showed a distinct dislike of England, and attacked British criticism of the United States. After 1825 he wrote a number of novels dealing with American history, such as *Westward Ho!* (1832) which concerns a Virginia family pioneering in Kentucky. Another historical novel was *The Puritan and His Daughter* (1849), about life in seventeenth-century Virginia and New England.

Two younger novelists and short story writers, among the best the nation has produced, began their careers in the second quarter of the century. They were Nathaniel Hawthorne (1804–64) and Herman Melville (1819–91). Hawthorne was born in Salem, Massachusetts, of an old Puritan family. After college he secluded himself in his home for twelve years and wrote. The first result was *Fanshawe* (1828), a novel that attracted little attention. His short stories, however, which were collected in 1837 in *Twice-Told Tales*, were more successful. Hawthorne was not a Transcendentalist, although he knew many of its leaders, because his outlook was pessimistic rather than optimistic, and he conveyed in his writing the burden of the decay of Puritanism as he saw it. His analysis of the Puritan mind pervades the tales collected in 1846 as *Mosses from an Old Manse*. That same year he received an appointment as surveyor of the port of Salem, but lost it in 1849 after the Whigs were victorious in the election. During this period he worked on his masterpiece, *The Scarlet Letter*, published in 1850.

Melville, born in New York City, was left to his own resources when young because of his father's business failure and death. He began his long association with the sea when he was twenty by shipping as a cabin boy to Liverpool. Beginning early in 1841, he spent eighteen months on a whaling ship in the south Pacific, but when he tired of it he and a companion jumped ship and had various adventures in the Pacific Islands. At one time they were captured by a tribe of cannibals, but were treated well. Eventually rescued, Melville served as an ordinary seaman on a ship of the United States Navy in 1843 and 1844. He used his experiences as background in writing his first five novels, which made him well known. They were *Typee* (1846); *Omoo* (1847); *Mardi* (1849), an allegorical romance; *Redburn* (1849), based on his voyage to Liverpool; and *White-Jacket* (1850), based on his service in the navy. Melville's popularity declined with the publication in 1851 of his finest work, *Moby-Dick,* which readers felt was too difficult and metaphysical.

William Gilmore Simms (1806–70) was the leading novelist of the South and was sometimes called the "southern Cooper" because of the style and subject matter of his books. The son of a poor storekeeper, Simms was never accepted by upper-class society in Charleston, but he remained loyal to its customs in his life and in his books. Among his popular works were *The Yemassee* (1835), a story of Indian warfare in South Carolina, and *Guy Rivers* (1834), set during the Georgia gold rush of the 1820's. He also wrote a number of novels dealing with the Revolution. Romance and adventure in a realistic setting was his formula.

Historians as well as novelists delved into the American past, and their writings generally upheld the nationalistic temper of the times. Among them were Jared Sparks (1789–1866), George Bancroft (1800–91) and Richard Hildreth (1807–65). Sparks, after serving as a clergyman and a magazine editor, became the first professor of history at any American college when he took that post at Harvard in 1839. He was president from 1849 to 1853. Sparks wrote a number of biographies and edited the papers of heroes of the Revolution. *The Writings of George Washington*, in twelve volumes, appeared between 1834 and 1837. Sparks's work made public many letters and documents that had not been available before but, in common with most editors of the day, he felt free to leave out material that presented his subjects as less than noble.

Bancroft was the most popular historian of the time, and his enthusiasm for Jacksonian democracy shows in his writings. His ten-volume *History of the United States*, which appeared between 1834 and 1874, was nationalistic and full of the spirit of manifest destiny, yet it was a more complete and critical work than any previous history. It was a success and his royalties made Bancroft wealthy. He was a successful politician, too. As collector of the port of Boston, he was the Democratic boss of Massachusetts, and in 1845 President Polk named him secretary of the navy. In his first year in that post he founded the United States Naval Academy at Annapolis.

Hildreth's point of view was anti-Jacksonian, which is reflected in his six-volume *History of the United States* (1849–52). It was accurate and honest in its appraisals and in some ways more scientific than Bancroft's history, but Hildreth's style was not exciting. After traveling in the South, Hildreth wrote the first antislavery novel, *The Slave; or, Memoirs of Archy Moore* (1836), which sold very well. It is an account of the adventures of an octoroon slave who escapes from a plantation in Virginia.

Two fine historians, William Hickling Prescott (1796–1859) and Francis Parkman (1823–93), devoted themselves to chronicling phases of the exploration and conquest of the New World. Prescott, although blinded in one eye and barely able to use the other, set out to write about Spain and Spain in America. The first such work, a three-volume *History of Ferdinand and Isabella*, took him from 1829 to 1838. It was well received and he continued with another three-volume study in 1843, *History of the Conquest of Mexico*. A slightly shorter *History of the Conquest of Peru* appeared in 1847 and two years later he began work on *History of the Reign of Philip the Second*. Prescott's history was accurate and he told his story with a dramatic sweep of narrative.

Parkman took as his field the long conflict between the British and the French for the domination of North America. He saw that his history would be the story of the American Indians and the forests of the eastern part of the continent. Parkman's health was frail and in

1846 he made a journey west, partly in the hope of improving his health and partly to study Indian life. The trip resulted in a classic, *The Oregon Trail* (1849), but Parkman's health broke down completely. Troubles with his nervous system and his eyesight made it almost impossible for him to write, but the first of his projected series, *History of the Conspiracy of Pontiac*, was ready in 1851.

Among other literary figures of the period was Oliver Wendell Holmes (1809–94) who, as a physician, in 1843 prepared a pioneering paper on the contagious nature of puerperal fever. Earlier, when only twenty-one, his poem "Old Ironsides" aroused so much interest and sentiment that it kept the navy frigate the *Constitution*—which had played a heroic role in the War of 1812—from being scrapped. His later renown for *The Autocrat of the Breakfast-Table* (1858) stemmed from the first two papers with this title which appeared in a magazine in 1831 and 1832. These pieces exhibited the polished wit and conversation of an urbane gentleman.

Richard Henry Dana (1815–82) interrupted his college years to sail as a common seaman on a merchant ship to the Pacific. For more than a year he helped gather hides in California to make up a cargo to be shipped back to the United States. His account of his seagoing adventures, a classic of shipboard life, appeared in 1840 as *Two Years Before the Mast*. Dana became a lawyer and in 1841 published *The Seaman's Friend*, a standard work on the rights and duties of sailors.

By far the most widely read poet was Henry Wadsworth Longfellow (1807–82). Longfellow was a scholar as well as a poet, holding the post of professor of modern languages at Harvard from 1836 to 1854, and was a leading figure in the social and literary life of Cambridge. His first book of poetry appeared in 1839, *Voices of the Night*, and others followed over the years. He wrote such favorites as "The Village Blacksmith," "The Wreck of the Hesperus," and "The Children's Hour." His long narrative poems, *Evangeline* (1847), *The Song of Hiawatha* (1855) and *The Courtship of Miles Standish* (1858) were equally well received. The last sold more than 15,000 copies the day it went on sale in Boston and London. *Hiawatha*, after selling extremely well the first few months, kept on selling at the rate of 4,000 copies a month for ten years.

Edgar Allan Poe (1809–49), both in personality and in writing, was as different a poet from Longfellow as one could be. Poe was left penniless at the age of two when his mother died, later quarreled with his wealthy foster father and tried his hand, unsuccessfully, at gambling. His erratic and troubled life included a short period at the University of Virginia. Then in 1827 he enlisted in the United States Army and the same year, when only eighteen, published at his own expense his first book of poems, *Tamerlane.* It attracted no attention. Two years later *Al Aaraaf*, containing more poems, was published and in 1830 he was admitted to West Point. He got himself expelled the next year by deliberately defying the rules. A third volume, *Poems*, containing "To Helen" and "The City in the Sea," was issued in 1831. Over the next decade or so, Poe worked in Baltimore, New York and Philadelphia as editor and author. He finally achieved some fame with his short stories and with *The Raven and Other Poems* (1845). In some of his short stories, such as "The Purloined Letter," he pioneered the tale of detection. In others, such as "The Fall of the House of Usher," he was a master of the macabre. Mood and emotion are central in Poe's poems and stories, his basic romanticism being tinged with melancholy.

William Cullen Bryant (1794–1878) was already a well-known poet when he moved from Massachusetts to New York in 1825. He wrote "To a Waterfowl" and other popular verses before he was twenty-one. From 1829 until his death, Bryant was editor and part-owner of the New York *Evening Post.* Although he continued to write poetry, Bryant's important work was as editor of this highly literate paper that supported reform movements, especially abolition. John Greenleaf Whittier (1807–92), born of Massachusetts-Quaker stock, led a busy life both as a poet and as an editor who fought strenuously for abolition and other reforms. His first poems appeared in 1826 and his first book, *Legends of New-England in Prose and Verse*, in 1831. *Voices of Freedom* in 1846 was a collection of his antislavery verse. James Russell Lowell (1819–91) of Massachusetts earned a reputation as a poet, critic, humorist and political satirist all in the same year, 1848, when he published *Poems, A Fable for Critics, The Vision of Sir Launfal* (a verse parable based on the legend of the Holy Grail) and the first series of *Biglow Papers*. The *Papers* were satires, written in Yankee dialect and opposing the Mexican War.

Two humorists whose work amused Americans were Augustus B. Longstreet (1790–1870) and Thomas Chandler Haliburton (1796–1865). A lawyer, judge, Methodist minister and president successively of four southern colleges, Longstreet was a man of the Georgia frontier about which he wrote. He was a good shot, liked to dance and to attend revival meetings. He wrote *Georgia Scenes* (1835), eighteen lively tales of the frontier told in a realistic manner. Haliburton was a Canadian who served a number of years as a judge in Nova Scotia, later moved to England and became a member of Parliament. In his writings, his character, Sam Slick, a traveling clockmaker, talked and acted like a clever New England peddler with more than a touch of western boastfulness thrown in. Haliburton influenced other American humorists with his series about Sam called *The Clockmaker*, three of which were published in 1837, 1838 and 1840.

The violence of the western frontier, real and imagined, was a popular subject with authors and readers. Charles W. Webber (1819–56) lived the life he wrote about. Born in Kentucky, Webber served in the Texas Rangers, studied at Princeton Divinity School, was a successful journalist in New York and died fighting with a filibustering expedition that was attempting to overthrow the government of Nicaragua. In between, he wrote novels exploiting violence, such as *Jack Long: or, The Shot in the Eye* (1844). Another was *Old Hicks, the Guide* (1848). Emerson Bennett (1822–1905) wrote fifty novels and several hundred short stories of adventure and intrigue, most of them with frontier settings. *Prairie Flower* and *Leni-Leoti*, both published in

1849, sold 100,000 copies each. The master of the frontier tale and the person most responsible for the "dime novel," which reached its peak popularity in the third quarter of the century, was E. Z. C. Judson (1823–86), better known as Ned Buntline. A trapper and a soldier in the Far West, Buntline was once hanged for murder but was cut down alive just in time. He wrote more than 400 dime novels.

Mrs. Lydia Sigourney (1791–1865), known as "The Sweet Singer of Hartford," was the busiest poet of the period and, next to Longfellow, the most popular. She turned out sixty-nine books and many articles from 1815 to 1865. Her verse was sentimental and pious, and much of it was lugubrious for she loved to write poems on the death of anything or anybody—from a public figure to a canary that died of starvation. Mrs. Sigourney was also an active worker for higher education for women. Just as prolific was Jacob Abbott (1803–79), who wrote about 200 books. The most popular were his books for boys, the "Rollo" series of twenty-eight volumes, the first of which appeared in 1834. Abbott's books were all very moral and taught proper behavior.

The years from 1825 to 1850 saw the start of the free public library system. Peterborough, New Hampshire, in 1833, used state-supplied money to support a free library and New Hampshire was the first state to authorize towns to establish tax-supported libraries. The pattern for this now universal institution was set by the Boston Public Library which was established in 1848 and soon became an outstanding example. In the quarter century, 550 libraries of different kinds were established, more than twice as many as in the first quarter of the century.

The intellectual and literary worlds at mid-century could point to a lively and productive twenty-five years behind them. If any one trend was apparent, it was the continuing Americanization of intellectual life.

17   Art, the Theater, Music

ART, THE theater and music flourished in the second quarter of the century, but in different ways. American artists still studied abroad but their subject matter became almost entirely native. The painters were strongly influenced by Romanticism, with its emphasis on nature, and they found perfect subject matter in the infinite variety of rivers, mountains, plains and other features of the continental-scale landscape. Theatergoers enjoyed British plays, actors and actresses, but it was also a time in which American playwrights wrote plays with New World themes and native actors were appreciated. Music was performed widely, even in frontier cities, but it continued to depend almost entirely on European composers and artists.

Romanticism and the American landscape joined harmoniously in the Hudson River school of painting, which appeared in 1825 and lasted for half a century. This school featured paintings of Hudson River Valley scenes, but it also included similar views of nature from the Catskill Mountains, Niagara Falls and the White Mountains of New England. Best known of the Hudson River school painters were Asher B. Durand (1796–1886), Thomas Cole (1801–48) and George Inness (1825–94). Durand first made his reputation as an engraver, then turned to portrait painting, including portraits of several presidents. He illustrated some of Cooper's novels. When he began his landscape work, Durand produced such typical subjects as "In the Woods" and "The Beeches." "Kindred Spirits" shows two of his friends, the painter Cole and the poet Bryant, standing on a rocky ledge.

Cole was born in England and on coming to the United States as a young man was much impressed with the landscape. He painted his first Hudson Valley scene after a sketching trip in 1825. Cole did such pictures as "Last of the Mohicans" (1827), "In the Catskills" (1833) and "Oxbow of the Connecticut" (1836). He turned to historical and allegorical subjects and still later to paintings with spiritual and religious themes. Typical of the school was Cole's use of rich coloring and dramatic arrangements, together with a diffused golden light. Inness was born the year the Hudson River school began and most of his work belongs to the years after 1850. He first opened a studio in New York in 1845, then went abroad in 1847. Inness's early work, such as "Peace and Plenty," was very much in the Hudson River school manner.

A double attraction drew painters to the Far West. The landscape of prairies, mountains and rivers offered almost more than even Romanticism expected from nature. In addition, the trappers and Indians provided fresh, colorful material for the brush or crayon. George Catlin (1796–1872) was one who felt this attraction and he became the foremost painter of the Indian. Although trained as a lawyer, Catlin taught himself to paint and in 1830 began eight years of travels in the West. Two books, published in 1841 and 1844, contained many plates of his renderings of Indians and Indian life. Most of his 470 paintings of Indians and tribal scenes are in the Smithsonian Institution. Alfred Jacob Miller (1810–74) also captured the look of the early west. He joined an expedition to the Rocky Mountains in 1837 and was probably the first artist to depict them. He also painted Indian and frontier life in general in such works as "The Trapper's Bride," his most popular work; "Independence Rock" and "Fort Laramie."

Carl Bodmer (1809–93), a Swiss artist, accompanied Prince Maximilian of Germany in an expedition up the Missouri River in

1832. Bodmer's eighty-one color plates were the main feature of the prince's account of his travels, which appeared in 1839–41. Bodmer was meticulous as to detail and left an invaluable record, as well as some of the most interesting of all paintings of the West. "The Bison Dance of the Mandan Indians" is an example.

Portrait painters continued to be in demand. Among them was Chester Harding (1792–1866), who practiced his art in a number of cities before settling in Boston where he became the fashionable painter of that city. He produced likenesses of a number of prominent Americans, including Daniel Webster and Henry Clay. Henry Inman (1801–46) was highly regarded in both the United States and Great Britain. He, too, painted well-known personages, including President Van Buren and the actress Fanny Kemble. Inman also liked to paint lively scenes, such as "Picnic in the Catskills."

Genre painting—scenes of everyday life—flourished and America produced two excellent practitioners in William Sidney Mount (1807–68) and George Caleb Bingham (1811–79). Mount's first contact with art was his apprenticeship to his brother who was a sign and ornament painter. He was not too successful as a portrait painter, but when he turned to genre painting he showed his true skill. His paintings, with Long Island as the frequent locale, are always lively and full of humor, as in "Bargaining for a Horse" and "Raffling for the Goose." Bingham worked chiefly in Missouri, where his family moved when he was young. Consequently, most of his paintings show frontier life, as in "Fur Traders Descending the Missouri" (1845), "The Concealed Enemy" (1845), with its theme of threatening Indians, and "Daniel Boone Escorting Settlers through the Cumberland Gap" (1851). Bingham's work, reproduced in the form of engravings, sold well.

Horatio Greenough (1805–52) and Hiram Powers (1805–73) were the leading sculptors, the former usually considered America's first professional sculptor, while the latter was the first to gain a reputation in Europe. Both studied in Italy and spent a large part of their lives working there. Commissioned in 1832 to do a statue of George Washington for the Capitol in Washington, Greenough produced a seated Washington, bare to the waist and draped otherwise in a Roman toga, with one arm bent at the elbow, the forearm and index finger pointing straight up. Some people abhorred this interpretation of the Father of his Country, some laughed at it. It was too large to go through the Capitol doorway, and too heavy for the floor. It stood outside for many years until placed in the Smithsonian. Greenough earned back some of his reputation in 1846 with another piece of statuary for the Capitol, "The Rescue," which depicted a settler saving his wife and child from attacking Indians.

Powers began his career by making wax models for a museum in Cincinnati. Later in Italy, he was strongly influenced by the classical sculpture of Greece and Rome. He produced the most celebrated statue of the time, "The Greek Slave" (1843), a nude girl in chains. Even though its nudity was shocking at the time, it was exhibited widely and small copies of it sold in large numbers. Powers also did busts, which were very popular, of people such as Calhoun and Webster.

Popular art was made widely available by colored lithographs, the sale of which was a growing business in the 1840's. The lithographs were hand-colored by women workers who received less than a cent each, and they sold at retail for from fifteen to twenty-five cents. Sarony and Major was one firm in the business, but the top position was gained by Nathaniel Currier (1813–88), who established his firm in 1835. He took into partnership in 1850 James Merritt Ives (1824–95), and the name of the firm was changed to Currier and Ives in 1857. Almost every subject imaginable was pictured in Currier and Ives lithographs: trains, boats, disasters, horse races, outdoor life, farm life and more.

Theater was popular, but most people wanted lively entertainment rather than serious drama. The large cities had numerous theaters and their own acting companies. Road companies toured the nation, although they sometimes did not fare well in small towns. At the start of the quarter century, New York took over from Philadelphia the theatrical leadership of the nation. The plays of Shakespeare constituted most of the serious stage fare offered, but an evening's program usually included several items. When *Hamlet* was staged in Boston, for example, the program also had on it a farce called *Village Gossip*. Special stage effects were an attraction, and managers tried to outdo each other. The use of horses on stage turned into a competition to see who could exhibit the most. One theater in 1837 claimed it used fifty horses in staging *Mazeppa, or the Wild Horse*. Shakespeare's *Richard III* was produced with the principal characters mounted. A Philadelphia theater in 1830 included an elephant and her calf in *The Forty Thieves*. An 1832 play called for sinking a ship on stage and launching lifeboats in a rainstorm.

The first American actor to become an idol to his public was Edwin Forrest (1806–72), who began acting at fourteen and first played *Othello* in 1826. He was a great tragedian although some people said he used his large voice to rant too much. He played *Macbeth* in England in 1845 but met with hostility from those who preferred the British actor William C. Macready (1793–1873). In 1829 Forrest offered a prize of $500, and half the third night's receipts, for the best five-act tragedy in which the principal character was an American Indian. The prize was won by John August Stone (1800–34) with *Metamora, or, The Last of the Wampanoags*, which became very popular.

Macready was one of the best tragedians of the English stage and gave excellent performances both in Shakespearean plays and in contemporary dramas. He made his first visit to the United States in 1826. During his last visit to America in 1849, the Astor Place riot occurred, on May 10. The riot grew out of the rivalry between Forrest and Macready, both of whom were appearing in New York at the time. There was an element of anti-British feeling on the part of Forrest's partisans, and they also represented the lower-class elements against the upper classes who favored Macready. In the riot the Astor

Place Opera House, only two years old, was wrecked, and even though the militia was called out, twenty-two persons were killed and thirty-six injured. The leader of the anti-Macready mob was E. Z. C. Judson (the dime novel author, Ned Buntline) and for his part he was sentenced to a year in jail.

The Booth family of actors began with Junius Brutus Booth (1796–1852), who gained a reputation as a tragic actor in England before moving to the United States in 1821, when he made his first stage appearance at Richmond, Virginia. He had a fine, rich voice and was superb in Shakespearean roles, but he had an erratic personality and was intemperate in his habits. Three of his sons made the theater their profession. Junius Brutus Booth, Jr. (1821–83) first acted with his father in 1835 and turned out to be a better theater manager and producer than actor. Edwin T. Booth (1833–93), one of the first truly great American actors, made his stage debut in his father's company in 1849. John Wilkes Booth (1839–65) was a proficient actor who assassinated President Lincoln in 1865.

The most popular actress to come from abroad was Fanny Kemble (1809–93). She was the oldest daughter of a British actor and manager, Charles Kemble, and made her debut in his company in 1829 as Juliet. The beautiful young actress was a success in both comedy and tragedy. She arrived in the United States in 1832 and two years later married Pierce Butler of Philadelphia, whose family owned a large plantation in Georgia. The marriage was a failure, largely because she hated slavery and could not stand life on a slave-operated plantation. She wrote a *Journal of a Residence on a Georgia Plantation* in 1838–39, but it was not published until 1863 when she hoped it would influence opinion in Great Britain against the South. She and her husband were divorced in 1849.

Charlotte Cushman (1816–76) was the first American-born actress of outstanding ability. She sang in opera when young, but lost her singing voice and turned to the theater. She made her debut in 1836 as Lady Macbeth and was highly regarded from then on. Miss

Cushman was excellent in tragic parts and played Romeo and Hamlet, parts commonly taken by women at that time. Her career was further enhanced when she acted with Macready in New York, and she made a number of triumphant appearances in England between 1845 and 1849.

James Henry Hackett (1800–71) and Joseph Stevens Jones (1809–77), both Americans, were highly regarded for portraying the down-to-earth Yankee type. Hackett made his debut in 1826 and his best role was in *Lion of the West*, a play by James Kirke Paulding. He was also a success in the part of Falstaff, which he acted in England in 1833, as the first prominent American actor to appear on the British stage. Jones's most popular role was as Solon Shingle in *The People's Lawyer*, which he first played in 1839. Interest in dramas about life in the lower ranks of city dwellers resulted in a number of plays in the 1840's. The style was set chiefly by Benjamin A. Baker (1818–90), an actor, manager and playwright, whose *A Glance at New York* (1848) was a melodrama that revolved around a volunteer fireman named Mose. Mose was played by Frank S. Chanfrau (1824–84), who was just right for the swift action of the play and who played the same part in other Baker plays, such as *Mose in China*.

Other successful American playwrights of the time were George Washington Parke Custis (1781–1857), Samuel Woodworth (1785–1842), Richard Penn Smith (1799–1854) and Robert Montgomery Bird (1806–54). Custis, a grandson of Martha Washington who grew up at Mount Vernon and was a planter, wrote as a hobby a number of plays with American themes, including *The Indian Prophecy* (1827), which was subtitled *A National Drama in Two Acts, Founded on the Life of George Washington*, and *Pocahontas* (1830), one of several plays about the Indian heroine. Woodworth, a journalist and poet, wrote the play *The Forest Rose* in 1825. Its comic Yankee character, Jonathan Ploughboy, was popular for half a century. He also wrote *The Widow's Son*, set in the Revolutionary period. Smith adapted foreign plays, including a number of French comedies, and also wrote plays with American themes. He was the author of about twenty, among them *William Penn, or the Elm Tree* (1829). He dramatized two of Cooper's novels and wrote *Caius Marius* which Forrest produced in 1831. Bird was a novelist as well as a playwright. He wrote some verse plays for Forrest, including *The Gladiator* (1831) about Spartacus. His romance, *Calavar* (1834), had a Mexican setting.

Anna Cora Mowatt (1819–70) was a writer of articles for women's magazines when she became both playwright and actress. Her satirical comedy of American social climbing, *Fashion*, produced in 1845, was a tremendous success and went on for years. She acted in it herself many times, although she first took to the stage in *The Lady of Lyons*.

When a troupe of French dancers performed in the United States in the 1820's, a scandal was created because of the flimsy costumes of the female dancers. However, when Fanny Elssler (1810–84) arrived in 1841 to tour the United States, she was considered sensational but acceptable, and was termed "the divine Fanny." A New York paper remarked on "the grace, the beauty, the purity, the hue of innocence and virtue." Miss Elssler was born in Austria and danced in Paris and London before coming to America. Her forte was folk dancing, and her performances were both energetic and sensuous.

Americans had the opportunity of hearing an increasing amount of music as the nineteenth century progressed, but on many occasions orchestras and other performers received meager public support. Several European orchestral groups, mostly from Germany, came to the United States in the 1840's and gave many people their first chance to hear professional orchestras. The Germania Orchestra, made up mostly of Berliners, arrived in 1848 and played 900 concerts all over the country in the next six years.

The New York Philharmonic Society was organized in 1842, and gave its first performance that December. It was under the leadership of a German-trained musician from Connecticut, Ureli Corelli Hill. Only he and the librarian received salaries. The sixty-odd members, mostly Germans, shared in the ticket receipts, which were small. In February, 1843, at the second concert of its first season, the Philharmonic gave the first complete orchestral performance in the United States of Beethoven's Third Symphony. The Chicago Philharmonic Society was formed in 1850 but lasted only four years. The first important chamber music organization was the Mendelssohn Quintette Club of Boston, founded in 1849. Choral societies were popular and were formed in Philadelphia in 1835, Chicago in 1842, New York in 1847 and Milwaukee in 1849.

Many Americans of the time learned to enjoy music because of the dedicated efforts of Lowell Mason (1792–1872). While in the banking business, Mason in 1822 compiled a successful musical anthology. He left banking for music in 1827 when he became musical director of three Boston churches. His collection, *The Juvenile Lyre* (1831), intended for the use of children in school, was the first of its kind. The next year he helped found the Boston Academy of Music, which enrolled 500 children in its first term and set new standards for teaching music. Mason urged that music be taught in the public schools and in 1838 he won his victory, becoming superintendent of music for the Boston schools, the first such position in the United States. Another collection of music, *Carmina Sacra*, which was published in 1841, earned Mason $100,000, an unheard of amount at that time. In the course of his long career, Mason wrote the music for 1,210 hymns, including "Nearer, My God, to Thee" and "From Greenland's Icy Mountains."

New Orleans was the only city to have a local opera company in 1825, and in 1827 it performed in Philadelphia and New York. New York, though, heard Italian opera in the 1825–26 season when the Garcia Opera Company appeared there. Lorenzo Da Ponte (1749–1838) was a pioneer in bringing Italian culture to the United States. The author of the librettos for three of Mozart's operas, including *Don Giovanni*, Da Ponte arrived in New York in 1805. He encouraged the Garcia troupe and in 1833 was a leading figure in the building of the

Italian Opera House which operated for its first twenty-eight performances under his management. Da Ponte became professor of Italian
language and literature at Columbia College in 1830. The first grand
opera written by an American was *Leonora*. Somewhat amateurish, it
was composed in 1845 by William Henry Fry (1813–64), who was a
pioneer in writing music criticism for newspapers.

A great variety of European musical performers visited the
United States in the 1840's and later. They came from several
countries and included sopranos, pianists and others. An unusually
popular visitor was Ole Bull (1810–80), the Norwegian violinist. He
made the first of several visits in 1843, and his triumphal tour took
him to New Orleans and the upper Mississippi River area, as well as
to the eastern cities. Bull traveled 100,000 miles and gave 200
performances. Strongly nationalistic, he played a great deal of
Norwegian folk music as well as his own compositions. In 1852 Bull
attempted to found a utopian community of Norwegians in western
Pennsylvania, using some of the money he had made on his tours to
support it. It was unsuccessful and the ruins of "Ole Bull's Castle"
could be seen for many years.

When the French pianist Henri Herz (1803–88) played in San
Francisco in 1850, the box office had to have scales on hand to weigh
the gold dust some of the patrons offered in payment for tickets.

18   Architecture, Science and Medicine

IN PRACTICAL matters around mid-century, American architects, scientists and physicians were highly skilled, although they showed somewhat less concern for the theoretical aspects of their professions.

Architectural styles were copies of older European styles, or, in some cases, adaptations of the more exotic architecture of China, India, Egypt and the Middle East. A building erected in 1847 to house A. T. Stewart's department store in New York City looked like a Florentine palace of the Renaissance. The showman P. T. Barnum built his dream house, which he called Iranistan, near Bridgeport, Connecticut. It was basically a large country house with a central block and wings, but it was decorated with bulb-shaped domes and minarets.

Two styles dominated architecture: the older Greek Revival and the newer Gothic Revival. The former, copying Greek temples with their columns and low profile, began to be popular early in the century. The style was used everywhere for public buildings and was also highly thought of in the South among planters building mansions. Although this Greek style originally called for construction in stone, it was easily adapted to wooden construction so that even farmhouses could look like Greek temples.

Robert Mills (1781–1855) was the architect who led the Greek Revival. President Jackson appointed him architect of public buildings in Washington in 1836, and he designed the Treasury Building that year. He followed in 1839 with the Patent Office and the Post Office. His design for the Washington Monument was accepted in 1833, but construction did not start until 1848 and was not completed until 1884. Mills's original design, besides the obelisk now standing, called for a base that was a Greek Doric Pantheon. Painter, engraver and engineer as well as architect, William Strickland (1788-1854) was another leading practitioner of the Greek Revival style. His most distinctive work is the Merchants' Exchange (1832-34) in Philadelphia, but his best-known work is the state capitol building in Nashville, Tennessee. Both Mills and Strickland were practical men and designed the interiors of their classical structures for efficient use.

Alexander Jackson Davis (1803-92) designed buildings in the Greek style, although he did not confine himself to that. With Ithiel Town (1784-1844), Davis formed the first American architectural firm of consequence. Town was best known for the lattice truss he designed which made it possible to build stronger and longer wooden bridges. The firm was responsible for state capitols in Indiana, Illinois and North Carolina, all more or less patterned after the famous Greek Parthenon. The Greek style was applied to a row of houses in New York in 1832, and Davis experimented with the first iron front on a commercial building in New York in 1835.

The Gothic Revival reached the United States somewhat later than the Greek Revival. Inspired partly by religious revivalism and partly by the ideals of Romantic literature, Gothic copied the tall towers and pointed arches of the Middle Ages, as exemplified in Europe's cathedrals. In America it was adapted to schools, libraries and even country houses, as well as churches. In contrast to the universal white of Greek-style buildings, Gothic used darker and deeper colors as more appropriate to what was considered the solemn and mysterious air of the Middle Ages.

The Gothic style, particularly as used in church construction, owed much to the work of Richard Upjohn (1802-76), who emigrated to the United States in 1829 from Great Britain. His first commission was for a house in Maine, and he then designed several churches before being called to New York in 1839 to rebuild Trinity Church. When this was completed in 1846, it set a style copied immediately by many other church groups. Upjohn did not confine himself to the Gothic Revival. A private house he designed in 1845–47 was done in the Italian villa style, with a square tower and overhanging eaves supported on brackets.

James Renwick (1818–95) ranks with Upjohn as a leading designer of Gothic style churches. He planned beautiful Grace Church in New York, 1843–46, and then was chosen in 1853 to be the architect for St. Patrick's Cathedral, also in New York, and the most ambitious structure of the Gothic Revival. Like Upjohn, Renwick dabbled in other styles, producing some buildings in the Lombard Romanesque manner, with round arches and usually constructed of brick. The earliest important building of this kind was the Smithsonian Institution (1846–47) in Washington.

The most influential architect and landscape gardener for country homes was Andrew Jackson Downing (1815–52), whose book on landscape gardening (1841) became the standard work and led to his engagement by President Fillmore to lay out the grounds of the Capitol, the White House and the Smithsonian Institution. His other two books, *Cottage Residences* (1842) and *Architecture for Country Houses* (1850), were equally influential. Downing contended that houses should fit into the natural landscape—the rocks, the slope of the ground and the trees. Accordingly, he designed Italian villas, Swiss cottages, Gothic cottages and English rural homes. Many of these were on estates along the Hudson River. After the firm of Town and Davis disbanded, Davis became associated with Downing and did many drawings to illustrate his books. Davis also turned to the Gothic style in his own later work. A prime example was Lyndhurst, a marble house with towers, turrets and archways, built at Tarrytown, New York.

American builders showed more originality in their use of materials and methods of construction than they did in architectural styles. The balloon frame method for building wooden structures was the most noteworthy invention. It replaced a method which used heavy posts and beams, some of them a foot thick, and which required skilled labor. The balloon frame method used light studs and joints to make a cage of boards. Diagonal pieces were usually placed in the lower corners to provide more strength. This construction required less wood, houses could be erected faster and by people of only moderate skill as carpenters. It is not certain who invented balloon frame construction, but it may have been Augustine D. Taylor who in 1833 erected a church in Chicago in this manner. American builders were among the early users of iron in construction. James Bogardus influenced future construction with a building he put up in New York City in 1848–49. The structural system of the four-story building consisted entirely of cast iron, except that the floor beams may have been timber. Windows occupied the area between the iron columns and the girders.

The construction and operation of large hotels with many luxuries and conveniences was pioneered by Americans, and the Tremont House in Boston set new standards which soon were copied. The Tremont was the work of Isaiah Rogers (1800–69), a self-taught architect, and opened in the fall of 1828. The first hotel with extensive plumbing, the Tremont had eight water closets, although they were all on the ground floor. Its ten public rooms were lighted by gas, and every bedroom had a wash bowl, pitcher and free soap. The Tremont also had a system of speaking tubes and a front office, which was a new idea. The Saint Nicholas Hotel, which opened in New York in 1835, was the first to cost more than $1,000,000 and it had gold-embroidered draperies. It was followed the next year by the Astor Hotel, named for its owner John Jacob Astor, and it, too, was the work of Isaiah Rogers. This was one of the first buildings anywhere in which mechanical equipment was a part of the basic design. Every floor had its own water closets and baths, with water raised by means of a steam pump.

Most of the major achievements of scientific investigators in this period were the result of work in Great Britain and Europe, while American scientists made practical use of advances in theory. Scientific education improved and scientific work was much more professional. Science was no longer the province of amateurs, but was the full-time occupation of college professors and government employees and was becoming specialized. When Noah Webster revised his dictionary in 1840 he found he had to add about 1,000 new scientific terms. One of the most important events in the scientific world was the establishment by an 1846 act of Congress of the Smithsonian Institution in Washington. The money for its founding, about $550,000, came from the will of James Smithson (1765–1829), an illegitimate son of the Duke of Northumberland. What to do with the money was debated by presidents and Congress for ten years before the idea of a general scientific organization was accepted. The executive head of the Institution was its secretary, and credit for much of the success of the plan is due the man chosen to be the first secretary.

He was Joseph Henry (1797–1878), a physicist who did fundamental research in electromagnetism. Independently of the British scientist Michael Faraday, Henry discovered the principle of the induced current, which is basic to the dynamo, the electric motor and the transformer. He produced an electromagnet that could support 3,600 pounds, and his electromagnetic telegraph made possible the commercial telegraph of Samuel Morse. Henry used the telegraph in 1850 to transmit weather reports and to help forecast weather—a service that led to the establishment of the United States Weather Bureau.

No scientific field was more popular than astronomy, among both amateurs and professionals. Denison Olmsted (1791–1859), who was an astronomer and a geologist, wrote *Lectures on Astronomy* in 1840 to help the general public understand and enjoy astronomy. The study of this subject, he said, was suitable "to the most refined and cultivated mind." Olmsted's geological survey of North Carolina in 1824–25 was the first official state geological survey. He tried to explain hailstones, speculated about the aurora borealis and made scientific observations of Halley's Comet in 1835.

John Quincy Adams was made fun of in Congress when he proposed that the nation build observatories ("lighthouses in the sky," he called them) to further the study of astronomy. A year after he left the presidency, in 1830, the United States Naval Observatory got a start when a depot for charts and instruments was established. Four years later, a new building for the charts and instruments was put up at the personal expense of the officer in charge, Lieutenant Charles Wilkes, and some observatory work began. Finally, in 1842, Congress voted money for a proper building, although nothing was actually said about an observatory.

An observatory was established at Harvard in 1839, with William C. Bond (1789–1859) as its director. Bond, the son of a clockmaker, became an expert in making chronometers. He was sent to Europe by Harvard in 1815 to study observatories there, and he later supervised the construction of the Harvard Observatory. A fifteen-inch telescope was installed in 1847, there being only one other in the world that large at the time. Bond studied sunspots, the Orion nebula and the planet Saturn. Bond was assisted by his son George Phillips Bond (1825–65), who succeeded him at his death. The younger Bond discovered the eighth satellite of Saturn in 1848. The Bonds pioneered in applying photography to astronomy.

Ormsby MacKnight Mitchel (1809–62), a West Point graduate, taught at Cincinnati College where in 1842 he established an observatory. He recorded his observations of about 50,000 faint stars, double stars and comets. Maria Mitchell (1818–89) was a teacher in Nantucket when she took up astronomy and studied sunspots and nebulae. In 1847 she discovered a comet and the next year she became the first woman member of the American Academy of Arts and Sciences.

Geology was advanced further than any other earth science and there were more geologists than any other kind of scientist. Edward Hitchcock (1793–1864) served as a clergyman before going back to Yale to study science. He was appointed the first professor of chemistry at Amherst College in 1825 and state geologist of Massachusetts in 1830. His reports on New England geology were very substantial contributions. For the last ten years of his life, Hitchcock was professor of both theology and geology at Amherst. In the South, William Barton Rogers (1804–82) conducted a geological survey of Virginia, starting in 1835, and with his brother, Henry, studied the whole Appalachian Mountain chain. Rogers taught at both William and Mary College and the University of Virginia, lecturing on a variety of subjects such as light, electricity, dew and meteorology.

The best known geologist, who was also a zoologist, was Louis Agassiz (1807–83), who was born in Switzerland and came to the United States in 1846 after having established his scientific reputation in Europe. He became professor of zoology and geology at Harvard in 1848, and was also a popular lecturer who aroused public interest in science. Agassiz introduced the laboratory method in the study of zoology, and developed a glacial theory in geology that explained certain land formations and the location of large boulders in terms of retreating ice sheets.

One of the leading botanists of the century was Asa Gray (1810–88) who taught numerous future botanists at Harvard and helped popularize the study of botany. His *Manual of Botany*, first published in 1848, was a standard work for a long time. Gray explored the West with John Torrey (1796–1873), a botanist who taught at the College of Physicians in New York and at Princeton. The two of them wrote *A Flora of North America*, issued in 1838 and 1843. Isaac Lea (1792–1886) was associated with his father-in-law, Mathew Carey, in

Carey's publishing house, but was primarily a naturalist. His specialty was the study of the shells of mollusks (conchology), and between 1827 and 1874 he wrote thirteen volumes of *Observations on the Genus Unio*. Prominent in chemistry was Oliver Wolcott Gibbs (1822–1908), whose studies of complex compounds of cobalt and of platinum metals were important.

American archeology began with the work of John Lloyd Stephens (1805–52) and Ephraim George Squier (1821–88). Stephens was a New York lawyer who traveled in Europe and the Middle East from 1834 to 1836, and wrote two interesting books of his adventures. When President Van Buren sent him to Central America on a diplomatic mission in 1839, he became an amateur archeologist and uncovered the existence of the ancient Mayan civilization. His two-volume work, with excellent illustrations by the artist Frederick Catherwood, was published in 1841 as *Incidents of Travel in Central America, Chiapas, and Yucatan*. Squier was a journalist and archeologist whose *Ancient Monuments of the Mississippi Valley* (1848) was the first study of the prehistoric mound builders of that region.

In oceanography and navigation, the nation owed a great deal to Matthew F. Maury (1806–73). Entering the navy in 1825, he was appointed in 1842 the head of the department that was gradually becoming the Naval Observatory. After studying ships' records for five years, he produced a wind and current chart of the North Atlantic that helped cut sailing times drastically. He and his staff catalogued 100,000 stars for use in navigation, and he also compiled a topographical map of the floor of the North Atlantic. Alexander Dallas Bache (1806–67), a great-grandson of Benjamin Franklin, was an educator and a physicist. In 1839 at Girard College in Philadelphia, Bache established the first magnetic observatory in the United States. As head of the United States Coast Survey, which he took over in 1843, Bache was in charge of mapping the Atlantic seaboard. When the job was finished, from Maine to Florida, an error of only eighteen inches was found.

The United States Exploring Expedition was probably the most valuable scientific contribution in the quarter century. The expedition of six ships sailed in 1838 under the command of Lieutenant Charles Wilkes (1798–1877). On board were a dozen scientists, as well as naval officers who were specialists in several fields. The expedition did research in the South Pacific and explored the coast of Antarctica, then proceeded to Fiji, Hawaii and the coast of the Pacific Northwest. In June, 1842, after six years, the expedition returned to the United States, having sailed 85,000 miles and circumnavigated the globe. Wilkes and his party visited 280 islands and sailed along 1,500 miles of the Antarctic continent. Wilkes thought he proved there was a continent there, but his view was not generally accepted until the early twentieth century. The expedition brought back 40,000 specimens of plants. Wilkes wrote a five-volume narrative of the trip and edited the expedition's report which consisted of twenty volumes and eleven atlases.

Between 1825 and 1850 some discoveries of great benefit were made in medicine, although epidemics of contagious diseases appeared regularly. Cholera and yellow fever were particularly deadly. Cholera ravaged most of the large cities in 1832, 1849 and 1850. The 1832 epidemic killed 500 people in Lexington, Kentucky, in one month and nearly as many in Richmond, Virginia. In 1841 and 1850 yellow fever was widespread, causing 1,800 deaths in New Orleans. Both diseases struck the South much harder than the North.

The finest boon medical science gave sufferers was the process of anesthesia for use during surgery. In 1831, all at about the same time, an American—Samuel Guthrie (1782–1848)—a Frenchman and a German discovered the properties of chloroform. The American Guthrie, who was a surgeon in the War of 1812, also invented a percussion powder and a punch lock for exploding it that made the flintlock musket obsolete. Chloroform was first used as an anesthetic in Great Britain in 1847. Crawford W. Long (1815–70), a physician in Georgia, used ethyl ether in 1842 while removing a tumor, but he made no announcement of this for several years. Two years later, Horace Wells (1815–48), a dentist, used nitrous oxide (laughing gas) in his work. He staged a demonstration in Boston in 1845 for the medical profession, but it was unsuccessful.

Wells's experiment was known to William T. G. Morton (1819–68), his former partner in the practice of dentistry. A physician as well as a dentist, Morton first used ether while extracting a tooth in 1846. Later that year he successfully administered ether to a surgical patient in Massachusetts General Hospital before an audience of medical men. An account of Morton's use of ether was written by Henry Jacob Bigelow (1818–90), a physician who was the first in the United States to excise a hip joint and the first to use lithotrity (a method of crushing stones in bladders).

The system of medicine known as homeopathy was brought to the United States in 1825 when Hans Gram, an American of Danish descent, opened an office in New York City. Homeopathy as a system held that most illnesses are caused by internal irritation, and that treatment with drugs that induce the same symptoms as the disease is the way to a cure—"like cures like." For example, since quinine given to a healthy person causes the same symptoms that malaria causes in a person with that disease, quinine should be used to treat malaria. Homeopathy's founder was a German doctor, Samuel Hahnemann (1775–1843), for whom the Hahnemann Medical College and Hospital in Philadelphia—established in 1848 as the Homeopathic Medical College of Pennsylvania—is named.

19   The American Home, Entertainment and Recreation

As CITIZENS, Americans were concerned with politics, with reform movements, with business and industry and many other activities in the world around them. As individuals and families, they were concerned with their homes and standards of living, and with the entertainment and recreation to which they devoted some of their free time.

Although the cities received an increasing number of poor immigrants from overseas, the middle and upper classes in both the city and the country prospered between 1825 and 1850. As they did so, their homes and their living habits changed. Larger houses were built, with rooms set aside for special purposes, and bathrooms were found in more homes. By 1825 soft coal was replacing wood for heating homes in cities, and in another dozen years or so anthracite coal was burned in stoves, at least in eastern cities. The kitchen fireplace was replaced by a range, and other fireplaces by iron stoves. Foreign visitors complained that American homes were too hot and that it was impossible to breathe the dry, close atmosphere.

Both the exteriors and the interiors of houses were less simple than they had been. Scrollwork decorated the outside and heavy furniture, with fringes on sofas and chairs, sat inside. This change was partly the result of the availability of cheaper factory-made household furnishings, from beds to rugs, wallpaper and tableware. The first wallpaper-printing machine was imported from England in 1844, and the first power loom for making carpets was patented the same year. Prospering families owned elaborate mirrors with gilt frames, many little tables loaded with bric-a-brac of florid design and, at the windows, dark and heavy drapes.

Americans ate well, at least as far as quantity was concerned, but the nation's diet was overloaded with heavy, starchy, greasy foods and lacked fresh fruits and vegetables. Every foreign visitor remarked, often with quite evident loathing, on the eating habits they saw. Mrs. Trollope said tartly: "They eat with the greatest possible rapidity and in total silence." Thomas C. Grattan, a British diplomat, noted that

> the national taste certainly runs on pork, salt-fish, tough poultry, and little birds of all descriptions. Two favorite condiments are cranberry jelly and tomato sauce. They form a part of every dinner . . . . Eating with the knife, loading the plate with numerous incongruous kinds of food, abruptness of demeanour, are the common habits of the *table d'hote*.

Miss Martineau reported she had a breakfast in Alabama that, besides tea and coffee, consisted of

> corn-bread, buns, buckwheat cakes, broiled chicken, bacon, eggs, rice, hominy, fish, fresh and pickled, and beef-steak.

Charles Dickens wrote of

> those dyspeptic ladies and gentlemen who eat unheard-of quantities of hot corn bread (almost as good for the digestion as a kneaded pincushion), for breakfast and for supper.

Advances in preserving food improved the diet of Americans to some extent. Two firms in New York canned foods as early as 1819, and in the 1830's the substitution of glass jars for tin cans made the process cheaper. By the 1840's canning was done on a large scale both commercially and at home. Improvements in cutting and storing ice made it cheaper so that by the 1840's a refrigerator became a necessity and was another means of providing more balanced diets.

Reformers were active in the diet field and an American Vegetarian Society was founded in 1850. Editor Horace Greeley at one time lived on a diet of beans, potatoes, boiled rice, milk and Graham bread. The last item took its name from the most successful of diet experimenters, Sylvester Graham (1794–1851). Graham was a clergyman and temperance lecturer who decided that proper diet could prevent alcoholism. The center of his diet was coarsely ground whole wheat flour. Graham's bread preserved vitamins that other milling removed, so he was right without knowing anything about vitamins at the time. Graham also advocated frequent bathing and open windows even in winter. His name became attached to Graham crackers and Grahamite health clubs and hotels sprang up.

The French Revolution and the Napoleonic era that followed set new styles in dress for both men and women in the early part of the century. Dresses were looser and hung freer; men abandoned knee-breeches for long trousers. But in the second quarter, styles reverted to drabber and more constricted clothes. Women wore corsets with steel or whalebone ribs that reduced the waist to as little as fifteen inches. Dresses were long, with many petticoats, while little girls wore pantaloons that showed beneath their dresses. Men wore long, dark jackets, broad at the shoulders and tight at the waist. Their trousers, also tight, had bootstraps. A light-colored vest might be worn, but high collars and large cravats made it difficult to turn the head. Hair was worn long, usually touching the collar in the back, and on the head was a tall black hat.

Professional entertainment was available to the public, at least in the cities, and none was more popular than the minstrel show, a uniquely American invention that got its start in 1828 when Thomas D. Rice (1808–60) gave the first solo performance in blackface in Louisville. Rice introduced "Jim Crow" as a song and as his impersonation of a Negro. When Rice went to England in 1836, "Jim Crow" became the first international song hit from the United States. Others followed Rice on the stage in blackface, and an entire evening's entertainment of this type developed. Daniel D. Emmett (1815–1904) and his Virginia Minstrels staged what was probably the first such performance in Boston in 1843. Emmett was a song writer who wrote the popular "Old Dan Tucker" that year and, in 1859, the even more popular "Dixie."

The minstrel show took on its full form in Christy's Minstrels, a troupe established about 1846 in Buffalo by Edwin P. Christy (1815–62). His troupe performed almost every night for ten years in a period when these shows were so popular that at one time ten were playing in New York City. The fully developed minstrel show consisted of a semicircle of white men in blackface, with "Mr. Tambo" (who played the tambourine) and "Mr. Bones" (who had bone castanets) as endmen. In the center was the only white face, that of the "Interlocutor," who was master of ceremonies. The first half of the show consisted of jokes, dancing, singing and instrumental numbers, and ended with the whole company doing a lively walkaround. The second half consisted of vaudeville skits and other acts. The best years of the minstrel shows were between 1850 and 1870, and among the groups performing were the Congo Melodists, the Sable Harmonizers, the Kentucky Rattlers and the Nightingale Serenaders. The white men who created the shows and the songs knew very little about the Negro or black music. As a result, the show songs were not west African music at all, but chiefly country music numbers; while the blackface interpretation of the Negro character made him cunning but feckless and ignorant.

Many popular songs enlivened the stage or the home parties where everyone joined in and the songs reflected events and attitudes of the time. Samuel Woodworth, the playwright, wrote the words for "The Hunters of Kentucky" in 1826 in honor of the Kentucky riflemen who fought at the Battle of New Orleans in 1815. The same year he wrote a sentimental poem, "The Old Oaken Bucket," which was set to music in 1834. Another sentimental poem, "Woodman, Spare That Tree," appeared in 1830, the work of a New York journalist and poet, George P. Morris (1802–64). Seven years later it was set to music by Henry Russell (1812–1900), a British organist who came to the United States as a traveling entertainer, singing his own songs, of which he wrote about 800. Among other songs of the time were: "We Won't Go Home Till Morning," "Zip Coon" (later called "Turkey in the Straw"), "Oh, We Never Mention Her," "Corn Cobs Twist Your Hair" (sung to the tune "Yankee Doodle") and "Go Call the Doctor, or, Anti-Calomel."

Although he was only twenty-four at mid-century, Stephen Collins Foster (1826–64) was clearly the song writer the public liked best. Musically self-taught, Foster published his first ballad when he was sixteen. His knowledge of blacks, who figure in many of his songs, came only from religious camp meetings and minstrel shows. Foster wrote many of his songs for Edwin P. Christy, allowing some of them to be published over Christy's name. Two of his memorable hits were written in this period: "Oh! Susanna," and "De Camptown Races." Foster never made much money from his songs.

Phineas T. Barnum (1810–91), sometimes known as the Prince of Humbug, was unrivaled as a showman. Barnum initiated his career in 1835 by exhibiting a very old Negro woman, Joice Heth, who he asserted was 161 years old and had been George Washington's nurse. Actually, she was about eighty. In 1842 Barnum opened his American Museum in New York where he exhibited freaks, curiosities, panoramas, wild animals, jugglers and anything else that would draw an audience. Among his attractions was the Fiji Mermaid, which was constructed from the upper half of a monkey and the lower half of a fish. Here also were the original Siamese twins, Chang and Eng. The most popular attraction, though, was "General Tom Thumb," a dwarf whose real name was Charles Sherwood Stratton (1838–83). He was only two feet tall in 1842, and never exceeded forty inches. Barnum made a triumphal tour with Tom in Europe, during which the dwarf was received by Queen Victoria. In all, 20,000,000 people saw him.

Barnum made a fortune of $4,000,000 out of his American

Museum, but his greatest single triumph occurred when he brought to America the "Swedish Nightingale," Jenny Lind (1820–87). Miss Lind, who made her debut in 1838, had a magnificent coloratura soprano voice. She arrived in the United States in 1850 and the advance publicity was such that 30,000 people surrounded her hotel hoping to get a glimpse of her. People paid fantastic prices for tickets. For her first appearance in New York they were auctioned at $225, but Boston topped that with a $625 bid when she sang there. Miss Lind gave ninety-five concerts around the country for which she received $176,675. Barnum made even more.

The panorama, the moving picture of the time, was another popular form of entertainment. A panorama was a very long painting, depicting some historical event or view of nature. It was mounted on the inside walls of a circular building or, if it was too long, it was shown a part at a time by revolving it on rollers. One of the best-known panoramas was executed by John Barnard in such a way as to seem like a trip on the Mississippi. It was supposedly three miles long and ten feet high and was first shown in 1846. Longfellow studied it before writing *Evangeline*. Soon another artist claimed a four-mile-long panorama. It is likely the longest one was only about 4,000 feet. Other popular subjects of panoramas were the burning of Moscow and the life of Napoleon.

Circuses developed into tent shows of many features when acrobatic troupes merged with menageries and equestrian shows from separate traveling units. In the 1830's, thirty shows were traveling around the country and one, called the Zoological Institute, claimed it had forty-seven carriages and wagons, over a hundred gray horses, fourteen musicians and sixty performers. A parade, heralding the arrival in town of a show, became an integral part of the entertainment. Floating theaters in the form of showboats, on the Mississippi and Ohio rivers in particular, began with the building of the first one in Pittsburgh in 1831.

The burlesque of the 1840's usually took the form of musical satires. Even Shakespeare was burlesqued, as in *Much Ado about the Merchant of Venice*. Plays that could be billed as "moral lectures" drew audiences of people who otherwise were against the theater. The most successful such play was *The Drunkard, or the Fallen Saved*, which in 1844 was the first play in the country to run for a hundred consecutive performances. Most daring among the forms of public entertainment were the "tableaux vivantes," or living model shows of the late 1840's. Scantily dressed men and women posed in such classical scenes as "Venus Rising from the Sea" and "Psyche Going to the Bath."

Cities were now large enough so that professional spectator sports events could be staged profitably, but development was slow because moral and religious restraints hampered some recreational activities. Partly as a result of the evangelical movement in the churches, recreation on Sunday was forbidden, even travel being banned in some places. Horse racing, a favorite sport of Americans since colonial times, was the first successful spectator sport. Harness racing, a purely American sport in which the sulkies were four-wheeled at this time, was dominated by the Vermont-bred Morgan horse, named for the founder of the line, Justin Morgan. Kentucky became the home of thoroughbred horse-breeding. One bluegrass country horse, Boston, foaled in 1833, ruled the sport for nine years; winning thirty-five of thirty-eight races, all of them two-, three- or four-mile races. When two highly thought of horses, Fashion and Peytona, raced on Long Island in 1845, it was estimated that 50,000 people tried to get to the track and some of them never made it because the traffic was so tied up. Peytona, from Alabama, won in two four-mile heats.

Baseball began in this period, although cricket exceeded it in popularity, and it was not "invented" in 1839 by Abner Doubleday, as legend has it. Baseball stems from the English game of rounders, which was played in America. The first organized team of which anything much is known was the Knickerbocker Base Ball Club of New York, organized in 1842. Three years later the members found a permanent home at the Elysian Fields in Hoboken, New Jersey, and adopted a set of rules. There were forty members of the club, consisting of professional men, merchants and white collar workers. The Knickerbockers played their first match game against another club on June 19, 1846. The game went only four innings and the Knickerbockers' opponents won, twenty-three to one.

Prizefighting was illegal and generally condemned for its brutality. Still, bouts were held, as secretly as possible, and the boxers fought with bare fists until one could fight no longer. In a bout that lasted three hours, one fighter, after being knocked down eighty-one times, dropped dead. When Yankee Sullivan and Tom Hyer tried to fight a championship bout in 1849, they were chased from one Maryland site by the militia and had to hold it in a woods. Boat racing was not only popular but also ranked high socially, and membership in yacht clubs was eagerly sought. More than eighty boats took part in one race in Boston, and Philadelphia had forty rowing clubs. A regatta staged by the New York Yacht Club in 1844 attracted many spectators on excursion boats and other craft. Professional foot races were staged and watched by as many as 30,000 spectators. The runners were called pedestrians. In 1835 in New York, an offer of $1,000 was made for anyone who could run a ten-mile course in less than an hour. One of the nine starters succeeded.

20 American Life: Cities, Immigrants and Other Matters

THE CITIES of America changed greatly between 1825 and 1850. In them lived not only many more people, including large numbers of recent immigrants, but also a larger proportion of the population. Urbanization brought other changes in American life—such as a new style of journalism—while urban and rural residents alike concerned themselves with nativism, phrenology, spiritualism and changing social customs.

The proportion of the population living in cities of 8,000 or more nearly doubled between 1830 and 1850: from 6.7 per cent to 12.5 per cent. In 1830 farmers outnumbered city dwellers by about 10.5 to one; by 1840 the ratio was only 5.5 to one. New York and Philadelphia were the largest cities, New York's population growing from 123,700 in 1820 to 515,000 in 1850, and Philadelphia's from 112,800 to 340,000. Baltimore in 1850 had a population of 169,000; Boston, 136,900; New Orleans, 116,400; Washington, 40,000. Newer western cities showed even greater gains: Pittsburgh went from 7,000 to 46,000 inhabitants between 1820 and 1850; Cincinnati from 9,000 to 115,000. Chicago, San Francisco and Detroit, which did not exist as cities in 1820, numbered 30,000, 30,000 and 21,000 citizens respectively.

The cities grew faster than improvements in the municipal services. The poor condition of the streets was obvious. Few streets were paved and garbage was allowed to accumulate almost everywhere. In northern cities, snow was piled high in the middle of streets and when, after being churned to mud, it froze again, both horses and people fell down in large numbers. As immigrants with little money settled in the cities, slum areas grew. Such conditions were offset to some extent by a movement, starting in the 1840's, to build parks and to plant trees. This came about partly because of Romanticism's love of nature, but also because it was thought trees would make the air better and prevent epidemic diseases which were blamed on "bad air."

As the largest city with the busiest port, through which more immigrants entered than any other, New York was noted for its hustle and bustle. Yet near the mid-century mark, the city had only seventy miles of sewers and did not create a sewer board until two years later. Hogs roamed the streets by the thousands, along with packs of wild dogs, while horse droppings put a stench in the nostrils and filth on shoes and on the trailing dresses of ladies. New York did not have an adequate or healthful water supply until 1842. In that year the Croton Aqueduct brought water in from about forty miles north of the city, to a reservoir located where the New York Public Library now stands. The new supply was badly needed for fire fighting. A disastrous fire in 1835 destroyed most of the old Dutch town. For two days in December it swept through seventeen blocks, destroying 674 buildings and causing damage estimated at $20,000,000. Fire fighting was in the hands of volunteer companies which also gave a good deal of their attention to fancy uniforms for parades.

Conditions in the poorer parts of the city grew worse. Between 1820 and 1850, the number of people living in slum areas in Manhattan increased from 94.5 to 163.5 per acre. An estimated 18,000 persons lived in cellars with six to twenty persons to each damp, unventilated room. Gangs of toughs, such as the Plug Uglies, fought each other and rioted. About one of each seven New York inhabitants in 1850 was a pauper, dependent on some form of relief. The reform movement included groups that tried to alleviate this suffering, although the approach was usually a moral one, hinting that laziness and immorality were the cause. The New York Association for Improving the Condition of the Poor was organized in 1843.

River towns and cities west of the Appalachians developed faster than others, and soon faced the usual urban problems. Pittsburgh led most other cities in providing a good supply of water. Its municipal waterworks, begun in 1827, pumped 600,000 gallons a day from the Allegheny River, and by 1830 had water flowing through more than 40,000 feet of pipe. Cleveland's population grew only from 1,000 to 6,000 between 1830 and 1840, but in the next ten years it shot up to 17,000. Cincinnati was the leading western city and one editor wrote that it was destined to be "the London of the western country." Cincinnati shipped 40,000 hogs in 1826, and in 1828 spent more than a third of its city budget on surfacing and cleaning streets. Chicago was the newest boomtown of the Old Northwest. Situated on the site of Fort Dearborn, it was not incorporated as a village until 1833, but in four years it officially became a city. It was a raw city where land speculation seemed to be the main business. Land that sold for $1.25 an acre in the late 1820's was up to $100 in 1832 and $3,500 two years later. Chicago also quickly became a shipping center for the products of the area, 600,000 bushels of wheat going east from the city in 1843.

Immigrants arrived in increasing numbers throughout the quarter century, except for a period when the Panic of 1837 and its aftermath discouraged emigration. In the 1820's the immigrants numbered 151,000; in the 1830's, 599,000; and in the 1840's, 1,713,000; a total of 2,463,000 in thirty years. In the decade ending in 1850, newcomers accounted for almost a third of the total growth in the American population, and by then one-tenth of the population was foreign-born. About 85 per cent of the immigrants arrived from Great Britain, Ireland and Germany, 105,000 Irish and 50,000 Germans coming over in 1847. The 1850 census showed nearly 1,000,000 Irish, constituting 42 per cent of all the foreign-born.

These new Americans came for a variety of reasons. Most compelling was the failure of the potato crop in Ireland in 1845, and for some time after that, which caused famine conditions. Political and social revolutionary movements in Europe, particularly in Germany, in 1848 accounted for a good deal of emigration from the continent. Sizable numbers of people also came from Scandinavia, Switzerland and the Netherlands. The bulk of the newcomers from all lands settled in the northeast and northwest. Most of the Scandinavians and Germans were farmers, although enough Germans stayed in cities so that by 1850 Milwaukee, Wisconsin, was, in effect, a German town. After 1837 Canadians, the bulk of them from French-speaking Quebec, added to the flow into the United States, although this migration was partly offset by Americans moving into Canada.

The regulation of immigration, if any, was in the hands of the states, which had to deal with such paupers, criminals or ill persons as might be among them. Skilled workers of whatever nationality found no difficulty in securing jobs, but the unskilled, mostly Irish, had more of a problem. Thousands did the hard labor of digging canals and laying railroad tracks. As more immigrants settled in the cities, crime rose, especially among juveniles, but how much of this resulted from the presence of unassimilated immigrants and how much was the result of poverty and slum conditions no one could be sure. The Democrats looked with more favor on the immigrants than did the Whigs. In the cities they wooed the Irish and built up strong support for Jacksonianism. The Irish entered New York politics with relish, and by the late 1820's dominated politics there through Tammany Hall.

A spirit of nativism—dislike of everything foreign—spread widely as immigration increased, and nativism became an organized movement that tried to keep America Protestant and Anglo-Saxon. The strongest feeling against the newcomers sprang from an anti-Catholic bias, but there was also the fear that the foreign-born would try to entangle the United States in the affairs of their homelands. The economic competition of immigrants was also feared, and there was a small element of racial snobbery present. Societies to propagate nativistic attitudes, such as the Order of the Star Spangled Banner, were formed.

Among the leaders of nativism were a number of people prominent in other walks of life. Lyman Beecher, at Lane Seminary, described a plot he was sure existed to send so many Catholics to the Old Northwest that they would control the region. Samuel Morse was convinced the nation faced a choice between "Popery and Protestantism," and between "Absolutism and Republicanism." Philip Hone, a wealthy New Yorker, wrote in his diary with a touch of both depression and snobbishness, that "all Europe is coming . . . all that part at least who cannot make a living at home . . . . not one in twenty is competent to keep himself."

An anti-Catholic mob burned an Ursuline Convent in Boston in 1834 and in 1836 an attack on nuns occurred in the form of a book. Maria Monk (c.1817–50) wrote *Awful Disclosures*, which purported to be an account of her life as a nun in Montreal. It was full of tales of misconduct, and although an investigation showed her story was false, many people believed it. When Catholics in 1840 demanded that state funds in New York be used to help support their schools, nativists were angered. Matters were further aggravated in 1841 when Bishop John Hughes insisted on running a Catholic ticket in the New York City election. James Harper, of the publishing family, was elected mayor of New York on a nativist ticket in 1844, a few months before a mob in Philadelphia burned several Catholic churches and killed and injured a number of Irish Catholics.

Nativism formally entered politics in 1843 when the American Republican party was formed in New York and spread to other states where it became known as the Native American party. The party's first national convention was held in Philadelphia in July, 1845, and delegates demanded that the period for naturalization be extended to twenty-one years, and that no immigrant be allowed to hold public office. Nativism grew stronger until the 1850's when interest subsided. The nativists were labeled the Know-Nothing party because, it was said, when a member was asked what the party intended to do, he replied, "I know nothing."

Journalism flourished and changed, aided by the increase in population and by the growth of cities. Technological developments in printing and the invention of the telegraph speeded up the gathering and dissemination of news, while the enlargement of the suffrage and the increase in education and literacy boosted the number of potential newspaper readers. There was also a leveling down in the content of the papers, and more space was devoted to crime, sports and sensational news events.

The number of newspapers increased and most new towns in the West had a newspaper editor on hand ready to do business as soon as they were founded. In the decade from 1840 to 1850, the number of daily papers grew from 138 to 254, and the number of weeklies from 1,266 to 2,048. In the previous decade, while population went up 32 per cent, newspaper circulation was up 187 per cent. Immigrant groups published their own papers and the *Staats-Zeitung*, founded in 1834, claimed in 1848 to have the largest circulation of any German language paper in the world. An important trend in journalism began in 1833 when Benjamin H. Day (1810–89) founded the New York *Sun*, the first paper to sell for only a penny (other papers sold for six cents), which put it within reach of the mass market. The *Sun* was also the first paper to employ newsboys.

The *Sun* faced a formidable rival after James Gordon Bennett (1795–1872) founded the New York *Herald* in 1835. Born in Scotland, Bennett came to the United States in 1819 and entered journalism. He started his paper with capital of only $500. It, too, was a penny paper and pioneered in printing financial and society news, as well as playing up crime. Bennett was the first to make extensive use of the telegraph for gathering news. He was also the first editor to have correspondents in Washington and Europe. The most influential editor was Horace Greeley (1811–72), the man who said, "Go west, young man, go west," but who remained in New York where he founded the *Tribune* in 1841. Besides the daily paper, Greeley published a weekly edition which went all over the North and West, and his editorials strongly influenced public opinion. He set out to publish a paper for the working class, but one that was cleaner and more intelligently edited than others aimed at the same market. Greeley, a liberal and at times a faddist, was always on the side of reform. As time went on, he devoted more and more of his editorial energy to the antislavery cause.

Walt Whitman (1819–92) was better known as a journalist than as a poet. In 1838–39, while teaching school, he also edited the *Long Islander*. After becoming a full-time journalist in 1841, his activity in Democratic politics led to his appointment in 1846 as editor of the Brooklyn *Eagle*, a post he held for two years. While he was in this position he began writing the poems that appeared in *Leaves of Grass* (1855). Moses Yale Beach (1800–68) bought the *Sun* from his brother-in-law, Benjamin H. Day, in 1838. He made use of carrier pigeons which he kept in quarters on top of the *Sun* building. Disturbed by the high cost of gathering news of the Mexican War, Beach took the lead with other editors in forming the New York Associated Press, the forerunner of cooperative news-gathering agencies. Outside of New York, one of the country's best edited and most influential papers was the Springfield, Massachusetts, *Republican*. Samuel Bowles (1826–78) began working on the paper, founded in 1824 by his father, when he was seventeen and took over control when he was twenty-five. The *Republican* opposed the Mexican War and was strongly antislavery.

Much of the humor of the time appeared in newspapers, and the writings of Seba Smith (1792–1868) were the most popular. Smith founded the Portland, Maine, *Courier* in 1829 and the next year began writing humorous letters, mostly on politics, under the name of "Major Jack Downing." The letters were written in a rustic Yankee style of speech and carried the implication that the common sense of such a character was the best guide to public policy. Other writers copied Smith, even using the Downing name, and cartoons drawn of Downing were the forerunners of the "Uncle Sam" character, representing the United States.

Periodicals for special interests were established, as well as others of a more general type. One of the earliest of the new magazines was the *Youth's Companion*, established in 1827, which was intended to be instructive and also entertained young people. *Godey's Lady's Book*, launched in 1830 by Louis A. Godey (1804–78), was the forerunner of many women's magazines. It printed material on fashions and manners, and was edited for forty years after 1833 by Sarah J. Hale (1788–1879). Under Mrs. Hale's editorship the magazine exerted considerable influence. She agitated for a national Thanksgiving Day so effectively that by 1858, all but six states celebrated such a day. Mrs. Hale was the author of the ever-popular poem, "Mary Had a Little Lamb," which first appeared in *Poems for Children* (1830).

A magazine for men, called *The Spirit of the Times*, was the brainchild of William T. Porter (1809–58). This magazine, beginning in 1831, specialized in stories recounting tall tales of the Southwest, some of which were collected in 1845 as *The Big Bear of Arkansas*. A magazine intended to interest the general public was *Graham's Magazine*, which resulted from a merger of other journals in 1839 under the editorship of George R. Graham (1813–94). Graham hired Edgar Allan Poe as literary editor and published works by Lowell, Cooper, Longfellow and other well-known authors. The *Scientific American* was founded in 1846 and published weekly. It was heavily illustrated for the time.

Among the serious journals, the *North American Review*, founded in Boston in 1815, was the most important and influential. The *Knickerbocker Magazine*, its name a tribute to Washington Irving and his imaginary character, Diedrich Knickerbocker, was a leading literary journal after its start in 1833. In the South, the *Southern Literary Messenger*, founded at Richmond in 1834, was also an outstanding literary publication. Poe was appointed editor in December, 1835, at a salary of $15 a week. His editing and his own writings helped increase the circulation from 500 to 3,500, but Poe was fired in January, 1837, for excessive drinking. In the West, James Hall (1793–1868), judge, banker and author, founded the first literary magazine west of Ohio, the *Illinois Monthly Magazine*, in 1833.

Despite the efforts of reformers on behalf of women's rights, the prevailing opinion as expressed by editors and authors was that woman's place was in the home, where the husband was boss. One writer solemnly said of the husband:

> It is his prerogative to hold the reins of domestic government, and to direct the family interest, so as to bring them to a happy and honorable termination.

And the *Young Lady's Book* summarized woman's place:

> It is, however, certain, that in whatever situation of life a woman is placed from her cradle to her grave, a spirit of obedience and submission, pliability of temper, and humility of mind, are required from her.

Many women's clubs were formed, most of a literary nature, such as the Edgeworthalian Club of Bloomington, Indiana, named for the English novelist, Maria Edgeworth, in 1841. Women on the frontier, however, were far too busy for such relaxation. One farm magazine referred to the "faded and broken down wife" of a pioneer farmer as typical. Rich or poor, though, the American woman had far more freedom than her European counterpart. Tocqueville noticed this (as he did the look "at once sad and resolute" of the western farm wife) and concluded that "the singular prosperity and growing strength" of the American people should be attributed chiefly "to the superiority of their women."

The steamboat and the railroad, together with the prosperity of the middle and upper classes, made possible the growth of vacation resorts in both the North and the South. Nahant, near Boston, and

Newport, Rhode Island, attracted many. The Catskill Mountain House, high on a ridge in the Catskill area and Greek Revival in architectural style, appealed to nature lovers, including William Cullen Bryant and Washington Irving. Saratoga, New York, won the title of the most fashionable summer place in the North, with enormous hotels such as the Congress House. Sea bathing, at such resorts as Long Branch, New Jersey, was a new recreation and mixed bathing was not fully accepted. In the South, White Sulphur Springs, Virginia, was the place to go.

A phenomenon of the time was the enthusiasm for the "science" of phrenology. Phrenology started in Germany around the beginning of the century and was brought to the United States in the 1820's, at first chiefly through the lectures of a Scotsman, George Combe. Phrenology taught that the specific mental faculties were lodged in different parts of the brain and that the development of each part could be judged by the shape of the skull at that particular position. Furthermore, phrenology taught that man could alter his personality and develop specific faculties of the brain by training. Orson S. Fowler and his brother, Lorenzo, were the leading popularizers of this "science" in America. Orson also devised the octagonal house, asserting that this shape was more practical and also imparted spiritual virtues. Many prominent Americans accepted phrenology to some degree. Among them was Horace Mann, who told Combe it had helped him in his educational work.

Just before mid-century, spiritualism caught the public fancy. Spiritualism held the belief, not new, that the human personality continues to exist after death and can communicate, through a medium, with the living. Spiritualism's modern development in the United States began in 1848 when two sisters, adolescent daughters of a Wayne County, New York, farmer, claimed they heard rappings on the floors and walls of their home and that the rappings spelled out messages from the spirit world. Margaret Fox (1836–93) was the central figure of this new cult, along with her sister, Katherine.

Margaret later admitted the whole thing was a fraud, saying she and her sister made the sounds by cracking their toe knuckles, but many refused to believe her confession. Andrew Jackson Davis (1826–1910) became the chief propagandist for spiritualism. He wrote *The Great Harmonia* (1850), which consisted of rambling comments he made while in a trance.

Americans also spent time expressing their patriotism in a variety of ways. One was in making an almost mythological figure of George Washington. An attempt in Congress to have Washington's remains removed from the tomb in Mount Vernon and reburied in the capital city brought on a bitter debate. The southerners refused to allow such a precious possession to be moved even a short way north. On the hundredth anniversary of his birth in 1832, Daniel Webster declaimed: "His age and his country are equally full of wonders; and of both he is the chief." The patriotic song, "America," was written in 1831 by Samuel F. Smith (1808–95). Smith, who became a Baptist clergyman in Boston, wrote it while a student at Andover Theological Seminary. The song was first sung at a children's celebration of Independence Day on July 4, 1831, in Boston.

Americans put their own mark on the English language, too, being fond of turning nouns into verbs—deed and portage, for example. The most distinctive contribution, though, was, "O.K." Some said the expression derived from the O.K. Club, a Democratic club in New York, and that the letters stood for one of Martin Van Buren's nicknames, Old Kinderhook. Another possible source stemmed from a Whig attempt to show Andrew Jackson as nearly illiterate by whispering that he used O.K. because he thought "all correct" was spelled "oll korrect."

Around the country from year to year, a miscellany of events attracted attention. A Rhode Island cotton spinner named Sam Patch claimed he survived a jump over Niagara Falls in 1827, but he met his death in the falls of the Genesee River two years later. On July 8, 1835, the Liberty Bell cracked while being tolled for the funeral of

Chief Justice John Marshall. A reporter for the New York *Sun* in August, 1835, wrote that the British astronomer, Sir John Herschel, had discovered that men and animals existed on the moon. The story was admitted to be a hoax, but not before some Yale scientists had been involved. America held its first world's fair—the National Exhibition—in Washington in 1845. Every state sent two exhibits which were housed in a somewhat ramshackle building two blocks long.

The United States was a never-ending source of interest to foreigners. Many came to observe the country and then went home to write about it. Most of them found faults, although some also found much to praise. Among many pointed comments were these by Alexis de Tocqueville:

> Americans of all ages, all conditions, and all dispositions, constantly form associations . . . . If it be proposed to advance some truth, or to foster some feeling by the encouragement of a great example, they form a society.

And by Harriet Martineau:

> I remember no single instance of patriotic boasting, from man, woman or child, except from the rostrum; but from thence there was poured enough to spoil the auditory for life, if they had been simple enough to believe what they were told. But they were not.

Mrs. Frances Trollope, English novelist and mother of the novelist Anthony Trollope, who while visiting the United States tried to operate a store in Cincinnati and made a complete disaster of it, wrote:

> Any man's son may become the equal of any other man's son, and the consciousness of this is certainly a spur to exertion; on the other hand, it is also a spur to that coarse familiarity, untempered by any shadow of respect, which is assumed by the grossest and the lowest in their intercourse with the highest and most refined.

21 The Compromise of 1850

EVEN BEFORE the Mexican War ended it was clear that the issues it raised would play a deciding role in the presidential election of 1848. The war hastened the split between northern and southern members in both parties over slavery and the acquisition of new territory. It also created military heroes to challenge the civilian politicians.

The contest for the Whig nomination was primarily between Henry Clay and General Zachary Taylor. Clay was seventy-one in 1848, and this was his last of many chances to reach the White House. Taylor, on the other hand, had recently returned home in triumph from his Mexican War victories. The Whigs decided Taylor would take more votes away from the Democrats than would Clay, so they nominated him. For vice-president they chose Millard Fillmore (1800–74) of New York. Lewis Cass (1782–1866) had little opposition for the Democratic nomination. Cass was a believer in manifest destiny and also in popular, or "squatter," sovereignty, which held that the status of slavery should be determined locally. The Democratic platform asserted that Congress had no right to interfere with slavery in the states. The Whig platform was mostly a statement of Taylor's military achievements.

Lewis Cass was born in New Hampshire, moved to Ohio when he was young and rose rapidly in the War of 1812 where he served under General Harrison. He was an able governor of Michigan Territory from 1813 to 1831 when he became secretary of war. Cass supported President Jackson in the nullification crisis. Later he was minister to France and then senator from Michigan. Cass approved of the annexation of Texas, was a leader in the fight to acquire Oregon, and supported the Mexican War.

The campaign was complicated by the presence of a third party, the Free-Soil party, with its motto: "Free soil, free speech, free labor, free men." It was made up of both Whigs and Democrats who opposed slavery, and members of the earlier Liberty party. Its convention in Buffalo in August, 1848, was attended by delegates from all fifteen free states and three of the slave states. The convention nominated former President Martin Van Buren to head the ticket and Charles Francis Adams (1807–86), son of John Quincy Adams, for the vice-presidency.

For the first time, by an 1845 act of Congress, the whole country voted for president on the same day in 1848. When the votes were counted, Taylor was president-elect with 1,360,000 popular votes and 163 in the Electoral College. Cass received 1,220,000 and 127 votes respectively. Taylor carried eight slave and seven free states; Cass carried eight free and seven slave states. The Free-Soil party polled nearly 300,000 votes, almost five times the number who had voted for the Liberty party candidate in 1844. Furthermore, Van Buren, by tallying more votes in New York State than Cass, kept that state from the Democrats. Otherwise the vote in the Electoral College would have been exactly reversed. The Free-Soil party elected one senator and thirteen representatives.

Thus Zachary Taylor became the twelfth president of the United States, but where he stood on many public issues was unknown. Taylor was a slaveholder, but was against secession. How to deal with the problem of slavery in the territories was the immediate and divisive issue, but Taylor died before it was certain just where he would take his stand. "Old Rough and Ready," sixty-five years old, spent two hours in the hot Washington sun on July 5, 1850, listening to patriotic oratory. Later he ate cucumbers and consumed a large quantity of iced milk. Stricken with acute gastroenteritis, then called cholera morbus, Taylor died on July 9.

The one important accomplishment of the Taylor administration of sixteen months was the negotiation of the Clayton-Bulwer Treaty in April, 1850. The treaty was named for John M. Clayton (1796–1856), the American secretary of state, and Sir Henry Bulwer, Great Britain's minister to the United States. The treaty grew out of rivalry between the two nations for control of routes for building a canal across the Central American isthmus. The treaty required that neither country obtain exclusive rights, or exercise exclusive control, over such a canal. The waterway, if built, was not to be fortified and its neutrality was guaranteed.

Millard Fillmore, who as vice-president had presided with impartiality over the Senate while it debated the slavery issue, began his political career in New York State as a protégé of Thurlow Weed and a member of the Anti-Masonic party. He joined the Whig party in 1834 and served in the House where he led the forces that enacted the high tariff bill of 1842. After losing the race for the governorship of New York in 1844, he was given second place on the Whig's national ticket in 1848 to please the Clay faction.

The debate going on in Congress when Fillmore became president began as early as August, 1846, when the Mexican War was only three months old. President Polk asked for an appropriation of $2,000,000, which he hoped to use to convince the Mexicans they should stop fighting and cede California and other territory to the United States. In the House an amendment to the bill, labeled the Wilmot Proviso, was introduced by David Wilmot (1814–68), a Pennsylvania representative who was strongly antislavery. Wilmot became a leader of the Free-Soil party and later a founder of the Republican party. The Proviso required that slavery be forbidden in any territory acquired from Mexico. Wilmot's amendment was adopted in the House but the Senate did not act before adjourning.

The following year, the Proviso was introduced again and, in somewhat altered form, again accepted by the House. This time it was voted down in the Senate and the debate left both sides angry.

Meanwhile, the governmental status of Oregon remained unresolved. The settlers there had formed a provisional government of their own, and President Polk urged Congress to establish a territorial government. If the wishes of the Oregonians were followed, slavery would be prohibited. It was unlikely territory for slavery, but as a matter of principle the South opposed any law against slavery. President Polk proposed that the line of the Missouri Compromise of 1820, at thirty-six degrees, thirty minutes of latitude, be extended to the Pacific. All areas north of this, which included all of Oregon, would be non-slave. Congress rejected this plan and finally, in August, 1848, passed a bill organizing Oregon Territory with slavery forbidden. Calhoun contended the bill was unconstitutional, but Polk signed it. With the discovery of gold in California and the rush of thousands of people to seek their fortunes, the problem of what to do about slavery there also became pressing. The Californians in the fall of 1849 adopted a constitution of their own which prohibited slavery and President Taylor in December recommended that California be admitted as a free state. Southerners fought this because it would destroy the precarious balance of fifteen slave and fifteen free states.

At this point, Henry Clay, having reentered the Senate in 1849 after a period of retirement, came forward with a compromise plan. He offered an omnibus bill with eight provisions: the admission of California as a free state; the organization of the rest of the land taken from Mexico without restriction on slavery; adjustment of the border between Texas and New Mexico, the former to withdraw its territorial claims; the assumption of the Texas debt by the Federal government; slavery to continue in the District of Columbia; the slave trade, however, to be prohibited there; a stronger law for the return of fugitive slaves; and a declaration that Congress could not interfere with the interstate slave trade of the South.

These proposals touched off one of the most momentous debates in the nation's history. Clay began it by begging both sides to moderate their demands to save the Union. He predicted that, if secession occurred, civil war would follow and that no war in history had "raged with such violence . . . as will that war which shall follow that disastrous event . . . of dissolution." The leading spokesman for the South, as he had been for many years, was John C. Calhoun, now a dying man, whose speech was read for him in the Senate while he looked on. Calhoun charged that the North had destroyed the equilibrium that previously existed by forcing a high tariff on the South and by trying to prevent the spread of slavery. The North must accord the South an equal right to the newly acquired western territories. Calhoun's speech implied secession if the South did not secure what he conceived to be its constitutional rights. Calhoun died less than a month after his speech.

The veteran politician, Daniel Webster of Massachusetts, spoke on behalf of compromise. This became known as his "Seventh of March" speech and is perhaps the greatest ever delivered in the Senate. "I wish to speak today," he began, "not as a Massachusetts man, nor as a northern man, but as an American." He urged tolerance on both the North and the South, citing the points at which he thought one side or the other was wrong. Near the end he declared:

> Let us devote ourselves to those great objects that are fit for our consideration and our action; let us raise our conceptions to the magnitude and the importance of the duties that devolve upon us; let our comprehension be as broad as the country for which we act, our aspirations as high as its certain destiny; let us not be pigmies in a case that calls for men.

Two men of a younger generation than Clay, Calhoun and Webster, men who were just becoming important national figures, also participated in the debate. One was William H. Seward (1801–72) and the other was Stephen A. Douglas (1813–61). Seward, born in

New York State, was active in the Anti-Masonic party, then joined the Whigs. He and his friend Thurlow Weed became the most important Whigs in the state and in 1849 Seward was elected to the Senate. He was strongly antislavery. In the 1850 debate Seward opposed the compromise and declared that there was a "higher law" than the Constitution, that is, there is a moral law or law of the conscience that requires obedience even if such action violates the letter of the Constitution. This speech made him the political leader of the antislavery forces. Douglas was born in Vermont but made his career as a lawyer and politician in Illinois, from which he was sent to the Senate in 1847 as a Democrat. He advocated "popular sovereignty" (although he did not use the phrase until later), under which the settlers in a new territory would determine for themselves the status of slavery in their area. As the debate on Clay's omnibus proposal went on into the summer, it appeared that it could not be passed as it stood and Douglas played an important part in the final compromise. He drafted the bills for organizing Utah and New Mexico territories, which gave the inhabitants the right to act on all matters as they saw fit, so long as their laws did not violate the Constitution.

In the end, Congress in September, 1850, passed five separate bills and President Fillmore signed them into law. Together, these bills made up the Compromise of 1850 and accomplished the following: admitted California as a free state; organized New Mexico as a territory and gave Texas $10,000,000 for abandoning its claim to any New Mexican territory; established Utah territory and gave the voters, as in New Mexico, the right to decide the slavery issue for themselves; amended the Fugitive Slave Act of 1793 to make it stronger; and abolished the slave trade in the District of Columbia, but not slavery itself. Reaction to the compromise was generally favorable in both the North and the South, although the southern "fire eaters," who wanted secession at once, were set back and the northern radical abolitionists were loudly unhappy.

The new fugitive slave act was the most controversial part of the compromise and the one that led to trouble. The law put fugitive slave cases exclusively under Federal jurisdiction and provided for the appointment of special commissioners who could issue warrants for the arrest of fugitives and who could also order them returned to their masters. A provision of the law gave these commissioners a $10 fee when they allowed a slave to be returned to the South, but only $5 if they refused. Heavy penalties were provided for interfering with the enforcement of the law. A citizen who prevented the arrest of a fugitive slave or aided him in any way could be fined $1,000, imprisoned for six months and be subject to civil damages of $1,000 for each fugitive lost by his action. Beginning with Vermont in the year the law was passed, a number of free states enacted "personal liberty laws," or expanded existing laws. These acts contained provisions intended to make it difficult for a slaveowner to repossess his property. In some states public attorneys had the responsibility of defending anyone arrested as a fugitive slave. In others, the laws provided that no public building could be used to detain alleged fugitive slaves. In some cases more extreme measures of mob action were taken to keep slaves out of the hands of those who claimed ownership. The South was furious, charging the North with bad faith and with carrying out unconstitutional acts.

Despite the seemingly irreconcilable conflict over slavery, the United States was expanding dynamically, both in territory and in population. At the end of 1824, the nation consisted of twenty-four states. Between 1825 and 1850, seven more territories became states: Arkansas, 1836; Michigan, 1837; Florida, 1845; Texas, 1845; Iowa, 1846; Wisconsin, 1848; and California, 1850. There were sixteen free states and fifteen slave. The strongest section of the nation was the northeast, the powerful industrial and financial area. Allied with the North was the rich, diversified farming area of the Old Northwest; while far away in California and Oregon were more antislavery-minded Americans who looked to the North rather than the South for leadership.

Population figures reveal the more rapid growth of the West and the North compared with the South. In 1800 the nation's population was 5,300,000. Half a century later, with the addition of huge pieces of territory, a rapid natural increase and large-scale immigration, the population was 23,192,000. In between, the census of 1820 registered 9,638,000; that of 1830, 12,866,000; and 1840, 17,069,000. Of great significance in 1850 were the figures which showed that the North now held 13,527,000 inhabitants, compared with the South's 9,612,000. The census of 1850 also indicated that 45 per cent of the population lived west of the Alleghenies and it appears that between 1820 and 1850 about 4,000,000 Americans moved from east to west.

In the operation of the Federal government, observers saw a trend toward the concentration of power and many people feared this. When it was proposed to establish a Department of the Interior in 1849, opponents charged that such a department would be dangerous. Senator Calhoun feared that "everything upon the face of God's earth" would go into it. The power of the presidency expanded, partly by the general course of events, but partly because of two strong presidents, Jackson and Polk. Such crises as nullification and the Mexican War required strong executive action. Polk was the first president to state openly the thesis that the president was the most direct representative of all the people because voters in every state chose him.

A large body of opinion believed that Congress had declined, not just in power and effectiveness, but even in manners. Some said the quality of Congressmen sank because of the spread of suffrage. In any event, Congress was poorly organized and this gave the president an advantage. As to manners and morals, the Senate purchased champagne for its members with government money and charged it to the stationery account until the president *pro tem* decided it would be more appropriate to charge it to the fuel account. One representative was known as "Sausage Sawyer" because he ate sausages while seated at the Speaker's rostrum. Misbehavior was not confined to the legislative branch. After Samuel Swarthout left the position of collector of the port of New York, a job he held from 1829 to 1838 on appointment by President Jackson, it was discovered that he had made off with $1,225,705.69.

Even if all was not perfect, the American people were making democracy work, under universal suffrage for white males. In spite of industrialization in the North and slavery in the South, both the spirit and the practice of equalitarianism held sway for the most part, although class differences had increased without doubt. Tocqueville wrote of the American people: "I cannot express how much I admire their experience and their good sense," while Miss Martineau thought they were "the most good-tempered people in the world." She attributed this to the fact that "forbearance" was a necessity in a republic, and at the end of her book summed up the Americans of the time as well perhaps as anyone could:

> No peculiarity in them is more remarkable than their national contentment. If this were the result of apathy, it would be despicable: if it did not co-exist with an active principle of progress, it would be absurd. As it is, I can regard this national attribute with no other feeling than veneration.

Reading List

BEMIS, SAMUEL F. *John Quincy Adams and the Union*. New York: Alfred A. Knopf, Inc., 1956.

BERGMAN, PETER M. *The Chronological History of the Negro in America*. New York: New American Library, Inc., 1969. Paper.

BILLINGTON, RAY ALLEN. *The Far Western Frontier: 1830–1860*. New York: Harper & Row, Publishers, 1956.

BODE, CARL (ed.). *American Life in the 1840's*. Garden City: Doubleday & Co., Inc., 1967. Paper.

BOORSTIN, DANIEL J. *The Americans: The National Experience*. New York: Random House, Inc., 1965.

BRANDON, WILLIAM. *The American Heritage Book of Indians*. New York: American Heritage Publishing Co., Inc., 1961.

BROOKS, VAN WYCK. *The Flowering of New England: 1815–1865*. New York: E. P. Dutton & Co., Inc., 1937.

BURCHARD, JOHN, and BUSH-BROWN, ALBERT. *The Architecture of America: A Social and Cultural History*. Abridged ed. Boston: Little, Brown & Co., 1967. Paper.

COIT, MARGARET L. *John C. Calhoun: American Portrait*. Boston: Houghton Mifflin Co., 1950.

COLLIER, JOHN. *Indians of the Americas*. New York: New American Library, Inc., 1947. Paper.

CUNLIFFE, MARCUS. *The Nation Takes Shape: 1789–1837*. Chicago: University of Chicago Press, 1959. Paper.

CURRENT, RICHARD N. *Daniel Webster and the Rise of National Conservatism*. Boston: Little, Brown & Co., 1955.

CURTI, MERLE. *The Growth of American Thought*. 3rd ed. New York: Harper & Row, Publishers, 1964.

DANA, RICHARD HENRY. *Two Years Before the Mast.* Garden City: Doubleday & Co., Inc., Paper.

DANGERFIELD, GEORGE. *The Awakening of American Nationalism: 1815–1828.* New York: Harper & Row, Publishers, 1965. Paper.

DAVIDSON, MARSHALL B. *The American Heritage History of Notable American Houses.* New York: American Heritage Publishing Co., Inc., 1971.

DE VOTO, BERNARD. *The Year of Decision: 1846.* Boston: Houghton Mifflin Co., 1942.

DULLES, FOSTER RHEA. *A History of Recreation: America Learns to Play.* 2nd ed. New York: Appleton-Century-Crofts, 1965.

————. *Labor in America.* 3rd. ed. New York: Thomas Y. Crowell Co., 1966.

DUMMOND, DWIGHT LOWELL. *Antislavery: The Crusade for Freedom in America.* Ann Arbor: University of Michigan Press, 1961.

EATON, CLEMENT. *The Growth of Southern Civilization: 1790–1860.* New York: Harper & Row, Publishers, 1961.

————. *Henry Clay and the Art of American Politics.* Boston: Little, Brown & Co., 1957. Paper.

FARB, PETER. *Man's Rise to Civilization as Shown by the Indians of North America from Primeval Times to the Coming of the Industrial State.* New York: E. P. Dutton & Co., 1968.

FAULKNER, HAROLD U. *American Economic History.* 8th ed. New York: Harper & Row, Publishers, 1960.

FEHRENBACHER, DON E. *The Era of Expansion: 1800–1848.* New York: John Wiley & Sons, Inc., 1969.

FILLER, LOUIS. *The Crusade Against Slavery: 1830–1860.* New York: Harper & Row, Publishers, 1960.

FRANKLIN, JOHN HOPE. *From Slavery to Freedom: A History of Negro Americans.* 3rd. ed. New York: Alfred A. Knopf, Inc., 1967.

GATELL, FRANK OTTO, and McFAUL, JOHN M. (eds.). *Jacksonian America, 1815–1840: New Society, Changing Politics.* Englewood Cliffs: Prentice-Hall, Inc., 1970. Paper.

GATES, PAUL W. *The Farmer's Age: Agriculture, 1815–1860.* New York: Holt, Rinehart & Winston, Inc., 1960.

GLAAB, CHARLES N., and BROWN, A. THEODORE. *A History of Urban America.* New York: The Macmillan Co., 1967.

GREEN, CONSTANCE McLAUGHLIN. *The Rise of Urban America.* New York: Harper & Row, Publishers, 1965.

HAGAN, WILLIAM T. *American Indians.* Chicago: University of Chicago Press, 1961.

HAMILTON, HOLMAN. *Prologue to Conflict: The Crisis and Compromise of 1850.* Lexington: University of Kentucky Press, 1964.

JAMES, MARQUIS. *Andrew Jackson, Portrait of a President.* Indianapolis: Bobbs-Merrill Co., 1937.

JONES, MALDWYN ALLEN. *American Immigration.* Chicago: University of Chicago Press, 1960.

JOSEPHY, ALVIN M., JR. *The Indian Heritage of America.* New York: Alfred A. Knopf, Inc., 1968.

KROUT, JOHN ALLEN, and FOX, DIXON RYAN. *The Completion of Independence: 1790–1830.* New York: The Macmillan Co., 1944.

MARTINEAU, HARRIET. *Society in America.* Abridged ed. Gloucester: Peter Smith, 1968.

MERK, FREDERICK. *Manifest Destiny and Mission in American History: A Reinterpretation.* New York: Alfred A. Knopf, Inc., 1963.

NYE, RUSSEL BLAINE. *The Cultural Life of the New Nation: 1776–1830.* New York: Harper & Row, Publishers, 1960.

———. *Society and Culture in America: 1830–1860.* New York: Harper & Row, Publishers, 1974.

PARKMAN, FRANCIS. *The Oregon Trail.* New York: New American Library, Inc., 1950. Paper.

PHILBRICK, FRANCIS S. *The Rise of the West: 1754–1830.* New York: Harper & Row, Publishers, 1965.

PHILLIPS, ULRICH BONNELL. *American Negro Slavery.* New York: D. Appleton & Co., 1918.

———. *Life and Labor in the Old South.* Boston: Little, Brown & Co., 1929.

REMINI, ROBERT V. *Andrew Jackson.* New York: Twayne Publishers, Inc., 1966.

SCHLESINGER, ARTHUR M., JR. *The Age of Jackson.* Boston: Little, Brown & Co., 1945.

SINCLAIR, ANDREW. *The Better Half: The Emancipation of the American Woman.* New York: Harper & Row, Publishers, 1965.

SIGLETARY, OTIS A. *The Mexican War.* Chicago: University of Chicago Press, 1960.

STAMPP, KENNETH M. *The Peculiar Institution: Slavery in the Ante-Bellum South.* New York: Alfred A. Knopf, Inc., 1956.

STOVER, JOHN F. *American Railroads.* Chicago: University of Chicago Press, 1961.

TAYLOR, GEORGE ROGERS. *The Transportation Revolution: 1815–1860.* New York: Holt, Rinehart & Winston, Inc., 1951.

TOCQUEVILLE, ALEXIS DE. *Democracy in America.* Several editions available, most of them abridged and in paper binding.

TURNER, FREDERICK JACKSON. *The Frontier in American History.* New York: Holt, Rinehart & Winston, Inc., 1920.

VAN DEUSEN, GLYNDON G. *The Jacksonian Era: 1828–1848.* New York: Harper & Row, Publishers, 1959.

WADE, RICHARD C. *Slavery in the Cities: The South 1820–1860.* New York: Oxford University Press, 1964.

————. *The Urban Frontier: Pioneer Life in Early Pittsburgh, Cincinnati, Lexington, Louisville, and St. Louis.* Cambridge: Harvard University Press, 1959.

WARD, JOHN WILLIAM. *Andrew Jackson: Symbol for an Age.* New York: Oxford University Press, 1955.

WEBB, WALTER Prescott. *The Great Plains.* Boston: Ginn & Co., 1931.

WEINSTEIN, ALLEN, and GATELL, FRANK OTTO (eds.). *American Negro Slavery: A Modern Reader.* 2nd ed. New York: Oxford University Press, 1973.

WHITE, LEONARD D. *The Jacksonians: A Study in Administrative History, 1829–1861.* New York: The Macmillan Co., 1954.

WILTSE, CHARLES M. (ed.). *Expansion and Reform: 1815–1850.* New York: The Free Press, 1967. Paper.

————. *The New Nation: 1800–1845.* New York: Hill & Wang, 1961.

Index